Galileo
and the
Magic Numbers

Galileo

and the

Magic Numbers

SIDNEY ROSEN

INTEGRATED MEDIA

NEW YORK

The author wishes to thank W. W. Norton and Company, Inc., for permission to reprint a translation of the ballad "L'Homme Armé" from Music in the Renaissance by Gustave Reese.

Copyright 1958 by Sidney Rosen

ISBN: 978-1-5040-6887-1

This edition published in 2021 by Open Road Integrated Media, Inc.
180 Maiden Lane
New York, NY 10038
www.openroadmedia.com

To Dorothy and David, for love

Galileo
and the
Magic Numbers

Chapter I

Galileo lay on his back, hands under his head, and stared up at the crack that zigzagged across the ceiling. There was just enough moonlight coming through the bedroom window to follow the dark line in the plaster. Outside, all about his house, the city of Pisa slept peacefully. Somewhere far away, Galileo could hear the faint clumping of horses' feet on cobblestones. It was probably the night watch riding through the streets.

On the other side of the room, his younger brother, Michelangelo, turned restlessly in his bed and muttered, "Good—good doggie." He must be dreaming of the puppy Father promised him, Galileo thought. His sister, Virginia, was still a baby and slept in their parents' bedroom.

The weather was cold—it was the middle of February—and the boys' bedroom was chilled. But Galileo was too excited thinking about the next day to notice that his blanket had fallen to one side.

Tomorrow, he said to himself, I will be nine years old. Nine years, that's a long time to have been alive. And tomorrow I begin my studies at the school of Master Borghini. I wonder what that will be like. Will he beat me if I do not know my lessons?

He remembered what his father had said about school the day before. Galileo had asked him, "Why must I go away to school. Father? Why can't you teach me more here at home?"

His father had shaken his head. "There are certain things I can teach well, son, and certain things I can't teach at all. Remember, going to school is a privilege—the privilege of nobility. The sons of poor commoners have to go to work by the time they are your age—there's no school for them. But for you, the son of Vincenzio Galilei, musician at the Court of Florence, there will be schooling. Be glad you are one who can go to school!"

And Galileo, who loved his father very much and would do anything to please him, clapped his hands and cried, "I am glad, Father, I am!"

Now Galileo began to practice his Latin declensions, conjugations, and grammar rules out loud, so that he would be ready for the next day.

"*Canto,* I sing; *cantos,* you sing; *cantat,* he sings. *Sum,* I am; *fui,* I was. *Qui, quae, quod, cuius, cuius, cuius, cui, cui*—"

"What is all this commotion in here!" His mother's voice hissed sharply as the door was flung open.

"I was just practicing my Latin for tomorrow. Mother."

"Oh, all that nonsense about learning and education! Better your father got some sense into his head and apprenticed you to some rich merchant! But these Galileis with their notions about nobility and learning! Now, be quiet, or you'll wake your brother, and then I'll have a job on my hands. You may be nine years old, young man, but you're not old enough so that I can't give you a good spanking! Now, go to sleep!"

"Yes, Mother." Why did Madam Giulia always have to be shouting at him, he wondered. I'll practice quietly, he decided. *Ab, ante, con, in, inter, ob, post, prae* . . . suddenly the words seemed far, far away. A moment later, Galileo was fast asleep.

In the morning, his father came into the room while he was dressing. Michelangelo was in the kitchen having breakfast.

"Inspection!" cried Vincenzio gaily. "Turn around! Point one—hose and breeches clean. Right! Point two—hair trimmed and combed. Right! Point three—jerkin clean and no wrinkles. Right! Point four—shoes brushed. No, *not* right!"

He pointed to a large spot of dirt on Galileo's right shoe.

"Sorry, Father." Galileo hastened to wipe at the thick-soled leather shoe with a cloth.

"Remember, you are Galileo Galilei, son of Vincenzio Galilei. We are a noble family. Remember that one of your ancestors was Tomaso Galilei, one of the Twelve Good Men of Florence. There are certain responsibilities that go with noble breeding: cleanliness, learning, good manners."

Galileo had heard this little speech many times in the last few years. But he loved his father very much. For Galileo, Vincenzio represented all that was beautiful and kind and noble in the world. He had taught Galileo the rudiments of Latin and Greek. And from him, Galileo had learned to do one of the things he loved best—to play the lute. After all, when a fellow's father is a music teacher—and good enough to have to make a special trip every week to teach at the Grand Duke's court in Florence!—the least a fellow can do is learn to play music well.

This morning, his father had brought his lute with him into the bedroom. "Well, just to cheer you up before you go to school, I'll teach you a new ballad."

Galileo took up his own lute from the corner and made ready to follow his father's fingering on the strings. One of the middle strings was slightly out of tune. He twisted one of the tuning pegs until the string struck just the right note.

"This is a noble ballad in the French tongue," said Vincenzio. "I will sing it that way first, and then I will translate for you."

> *L'homme, l'homme, l'homme armé,*
> *L'homme armé, l'homme armé doibt on doubter, doibt*
> *on doubter,*
> *On a fait partout crier:*
> *Que chascun se veigne armer*
> *D'un haubregon de fer!*

"That's a very fetching tune. It makes me feel like marching. What do the words mean?"

"This ballad is a humorous one, describing how the people feel about knights in armor."

> *Oh, the man, the man, the man at arms,*
> *He fills us all with dread alarms;*
> *Everywhere, the people wail:*
> *Find, if you would breast the gale,*
> *A good stout coat of mail!*

Galileo and Vincenzio played the music over together, and then sang the whole ballad through once. Not a mistake. Vincenzio was very proud of his son.

"Are you two lazy fellows going to spend the whole day in that bedroom? The breakfast is cold. It is almost eight o'clock. That son of yours will be late for his precious lessons, Vincenzio!"

Why does she have to scold so? Galileo felt annoyed with his mother. Her fit of bad temper was nothing new. As far back as he could remember, Galileo had heard his mother's voice raised in shrill argument. She screamed at Vincenzio about the lack of money in the house. She nagged at the children day and night about a thousand different little things.

Why couldn't I have a mother who is kind and pleasant like my father? thought Galileo. But then he suddenly remembered a night a few months before, when he had lain in his bed burning and tossing with fever. His mother had sat beside him all night, not sleeping, soothing and cooling him as best she could. His scolding mother could be a kind and loving angel at the right moments.

Galileo sighed. He and Vincenzio went sheepishly to eat their cold breakfast.

It was time to leave for Signor Borghini's house. Galileo excused himself from the table and went for his woolen coat, a hand-me-down that was almost threadbare. The coat was gone! Galileo ran back to the dining room.

"Something wrong?" asked his father.

"My coat—my coat—it's—it's—"

Michelangelo mocked him: "It's—it's—"

Vincenzio laughed. "Oh, that old thing! I gave that to a beggar yesterday."

"Then I cannot go to school?"

"Look in the corner there."

Galileo turned. Hanging on a hook on the wall was the most beautiful winter cape he had ever seen, made in the Spanish style. The collar was cut square and stood partly erect; its edge was trimmed with soft fur.

"Happy birthday, Galileo!" cried Vincenzio and Madam Giulia and Michelangelo. Even the baby, Virginia, though she could not yet speak, gurgled and clapped her hands to show that she wanted to play the game too.

Vincenzio placed the cloak about Galileo's shoulders. It fitted perfectly. "Well, look at our handsome little nobleman now!"

"I want a birthday present, too!" cried Michelangelo. Vincenzio tried to explain to him that he would get a present when his birthday came, but to no avail. Michelangelo cried and fussed and had to be sent out of the room.

"I must admit Galileo looks elegant," sighed Madam Giulia, "but it's such an expensive coat."

"A present from a nobleman at the Florentine Court. I gave his son a lute lesson or two. Naturally, he was grateful."

"Naturally, I would have been more grateful for a few gold florins for food and better clothing for all of us!"

"Ah, stop nagging, woman!" shouted Vincenzio.

"Why don't you find a more generous patron, then? This one squeezes a florin ten times before it leaves his fingers!"

Galileo was embarrassed by the argument. He tried to change the subject. "What does Mother mean by a patron?" he asked his father.

Vincenzio appeared a little abashed. "Well, a patron is like a—well, like a protector. In these times, painters and musicians and writers look to some wealthy nobleman to support them while they create works of art."

"Just a fancy way of begging!" put in Madam Giulia.

"That is not true! It's just the way of the times, that is all. Otherwise, artists would starve, and there would be no great paintings, no beautiful music, no magnificent statues, no books. You understand, Galileo?"

"Yes, Father, I understand."

"There is no shame connected with patronage, as your mother would have you believe. Well, that's enough of that. Here are your books. Off with you, my boy!"

Galileo, pretending he was a grand duke, with head and nose high in the air, minced past his parents and out the front door. His father roared with laughter, and even his mother couldn't help giggling. For a nine-year-old, their son had a fine sense of humor.

Master Jacopo Borghini was a small dried-up man, upon whose thin and wrinkled face sat immeasurable sadness. He took Galileo's new cloak and gazed at it a moment before he hung it up.

"Noble clothing, eh? Well, I'm more concerned with new ideas in the head than I am with new clothes on the back. Now, tell me: how far have you gone in your Latin?"

For the next thirty minutes, Borghini quizzed Galileo closely on Latin forms and grammar. The Latin went well. Next came Greek. This didn't take as long, because Vincenzio's understanding of Greek had been rather poor.

"Well, we'll have to work on that Greek grammar. Now, how about mathematics?"

"Mathematics? You mean arithmetic? I can add and subtract numbers."

"Do you know Pythagorean number magic?"

Galileo shook his head. He knew about witches and black magic, but number magic—? That was a new kind of magic.

Borghini went to the cupboard and returned with a handful of little white pebbles.

"Pythagoras was a Greek philosopher who lived over two thousand years ago. He loved numbers. For him, the whole universe could be explained by mathematics. He thought numbers could describe beauty, music, and even the acts of gods and men. Your father is a musician, is he not?"

"Yes, Master, and a fine one."

"So I am told. Then you will understand what I mean when I say that Pythagoras invented the first numbered musical scale."

"He must have been a very great man, indeed, to have done that."

Master Jacopo knelt on the floor and motioned Galileo to do the same. Galileo's eyes widened. This was a strange way for a teacher to act! Most of his friends had told him dreadful stories of their teachers. They all insisted upon strict discipline and were very formal and stiff. Yet this teacher was asking him to sit on the floor to play games! Galileo sat, legs crossed like a Saracen.

'Now, this is the magic," said Borghini. He placed one pebble on the floor.

'What number is that?"

"One!"

"Now I make a triangle by adding two pebbles. A triangle is a figure with three sides. Observe."

"What number now?"

"Three!"

Master Jacopo added three pebbles. The triangle grew larger.

"That makes six!"

Now the triangle became very large, as four pebbles were added.

"That makes ten!"

"Correct. Now, what were the first three triangles?"

"I remember. One and three and six." Galileo's eyebrows rose in excitement. "But that adds up to ten!"

"That is the magic. Master Galileo. The first three triangles add up to make the fourth one. And each time, we added only one more pebble than the previous time!"

For some reason he could not understand, Galileo thought this was the most wonderful thing he had ever learned! And when Master Jacopo arose, dusted off his hose, pat away the pebbles, and said, "Now for those Greek conjugations," Galileo was reluctant to move.

But when Borghini added, "Perhaps tomorrow will bring another kind of number magic," Galileo leaped to his feet. He was ready to struggle with dull Latin or Greek—as long as there was promise of more Pythagorean games.

Almost a year and a half passed. Galileo came home one day to find the house in an uproar. Everything had been taken off the pantry shelves, and all the closets had been emptied. Clothing was strewn over tables and chairs. In the center of the kitchen, Madam Giulia was packing dishes into a large cask; with the other hand, she fended off little Virginia, who kept getting in her way. Madam Giulia's face was red from exertion, and her breath came in gasps.

"Get away—you pestiferous child—go away and play—a plague on this packing—Michelangelo! Michelangelo!"

Galileo's brother came running in from the bedroom.

"Take your sister out of doors and play with her. Do something, anything, but get her out of my way!"

Michelangelo picked up Virginia. The little girl laughed happily at what she thought was a wonderful game. Michelangelo, laughing and teasing, carried her outside.

"Are we moving away. Mother?" asked Galileo.

"No, of course not, this is a game I'm playing," scolded his mother. Then she looked up and saw the surprise on Galileo's face. "Glory to heaven, didn't you know? Your father again! He forgot to tell you this morning. We're moving to Florence!"

"To Florence!" Galileo's eyes brightened. What an adventure! Florence was the center of Tuscany, where the leading noble family, the Medici, lived in their marble palaces. Florence was the great city, full of wonderful people, wonderful streets, wonderful things! In Florence, there lived famous painters and sculptors. Galileo had heard of one, a man named Leonardo da Vinci. This man had invented huge machines of war and had painted many beautiful pictures. It was said of him that he had made a machine that would enable a man to fly like a bird!

Galileo loved to make little toys that moved of themselves. He made, of sticks and little flat stones, a windmill that moved and really ground little kernels of wheat into flour. He made a sailboat that steered itself across a rainwater puddle. But a machine that had wings and flew like a bird! That was the invention of a great master!

"Well, don't stand there like an idiot! Get a box and begin to pack your things!"

"Why are we going to Florence?" asked Galileo, starting from his dream about Leonardo.

"You know your father teaches music at the court! Now it is to be a full-time position, and no more week-end traveling! The pay isn't much, but at least it will be steady. So, we are moving into a house in Florence. Now, hurry; we leave the first thing in the morning!"

Galileo made ready the little clothing he had and the few possessions that were his very own—his books, his lute, the little windmill that ground wheat, a drawing he had made of the Leaning Tower, and a small bag full of round pebbles. These last had become most precious, for with them he had practiced the number magic of Pythagoras.

"Well, boy, don't just sit there staring into space. Get a move on with your packing!" Galileo's father came into the room. "Are you glad to be going to Florence?"

"Yes, Father. You know, every day, as I crossed over the Arno River to go to school, I used to look up the river to the east and think: there is the great city of Florence, where my father teaches noble lords and ladies to play the lute. Some day, I shall go there myself and see all the great palaces and the noble people. And now we are going, and I shall see them!"

Vincenzio ruffled his son's hair. "Not if you don't hustle with that packing. And when you're through, give your mother a hand, or she'll have our hide!" He winked conspiratorially at Galileo.

At sunrise the next morning, a cart stood before the door. The day promised to be cloudless and warm—a good omen. Galileo awoke to the sound of men's voices.

"I think ten florins is not too high for such a load!"

"Ten florins! Man, what are you thinking of? This isn't the Grand Duke of Tuscany you're moving. We'll give you six!"

Galileo recognized his uncle, Muzio Tedaldi, who had promised to come and help with the moving. The other voice apparently belonged to the wagoner who was to drive them to Florence.

Six! It's hardly worth it!"

"Muzio! Guido! What's all this wrangling?" He heard his father intervene. "Let's settle it for eight florins. Agreed?"

"Too much!" cried Muzio. But the wagoner muttered, "Agreed!" A moment later, the three men were laughing together at a joke Vincenzio had made. How wonderful it was to have a father who could settle disputes so wisely!

Galileo leaped out of bed, awakened Michelangelo, and threw his clothing on in a frenzy. He felt almost delirious with excitement and joy.

The wagon was soon filled with the meager possessions of the Galilei family, and the simple breakfast was quickly eaten. Vincenzio helped Madam Giulia up into the wagon, and then tossed Virginia up to her. He lifted Michelangelo and swung him up beside his mother.

"All present and accounted for? Then off we go!"

The wagoner cracked his whip, the horse strained at the harness, and away they went. Galileo sat facing Pisa and waving good-by to his uncle. Soon, Signor Tedaldi was only a little speck, almost hidden by the dust of the road. Galileo turned around.

Out there before them, the road ran eastward all the way to the great, splendid city of Florence. Vincenzio had already taken up his lute and was singing.

> *L'homme, L'homme, L'homme armé, L'homme armé,*
> *L'homme armé doibt on doubter—*

As loudly as he could, Galileo joined in. Their voices rang out over the rumbling of the wheels, as the little wagon rattled along the dusty road to Florence.

Chapter II

It took Galileo a little time to get used to the great city of Florence. It was much larger than Pisa, and much dirtier; and living was more dangerous. Handsome gilded carriages drawn by fine horses dashed through the streets; the crowds in the wide squares jostled and pushed without regard for life or limb; the streets at night were filled with pickpockets.

Galileo missed the smell of the sea. In Pisa, the fresh, salty odor filled one's nostrils as the wind blew in from the harbor up the river. Florence was too far away from the mouth of the Arno for the sea smell to reach. And for a while, Galileo was very lonely, for he had no friends.

He played with Michelangelo and Virginia. But Michelangelo was getting to be a very spoiled and quarrelsome boy. When Galileo built a sailboat, so that they could play the game of "sailing to the Indies" in the stream of water that ran down the gutter of their street, Michelangelo would want to be captain always. If Galileo disagreed, his brother would snatch the boat and break it to pieces. Then he would run crying to his mother. She petted and soothed him, and scolded Galileo. Virginia was a good little girl, but she always wanted to "play house." He soon tired of that game.

Galileo began to spend more time reading. Books were too expensive for poor people to acquire. The money of the Galilei family went for food, clothing, and house rent. There was little extra left for such luxuries as books. Vincenzio, however, managed to borrow books for Galileo from some of the rich noblemen of the court. Most of the books were in Latin or Greek, and Galileo found them difficult to read, in spite of Master Borghini's teaching.

Whenever Vincenzio was home, he would spend most of his time helping Galileo to improve his lute playing. There were two other instruments in the house, a viola da gamba and a small organ. The viola was a large stringed instrument, something like a great overstuffed violin. It was held between the legs and played with a bow drawn gently over the strings. After a few months, Galileo could play the viola very well.

There was one song that Galileo loved to play on the viola da gamba while his father sang. It was a sad madrigal, and the soft low tones of the strings just matched the mood of the music.

> *The soft white swan dies singing,*
> *And, weeping, I come to the end of my life.*

And, as his father's voice faded away on the last note, Galileo struggled to keep his eyes from stinging with tears. He didn't really understand what the song said, but he knew it was very lovely and sad.

The organ was harder to play. It required the use of both hands. But Vincenzio was a patient teacher. After a while, Galileo could play the lute, the viola, and the organ with equal skill. But the lute was his favorite instrument.

Madam Giulia took dim notice of these goings on. "What kind of nonsense are you putting into that boy's head,

Vincenzio? Will he get rich rubbing hair from a horse's tail over that fat fiddle? Will he be able to provide for us in our old age by twanging lute strings all his life? How many gold pieces a week will people give him for banging away at that organ? When are you going to see that he learns a decent and paying trade?"

On this point, Vincenzio was very stubborn. He would purse his lips tightly, draw himself up to his full height, and tell Madam Giulia, "You forget that you are of a noble family, Giulia. The sons of the Galilei will learn what is proper for noble youths to learn. Latin, Greek, music, and art—these are proper subjects. He will find his place in life when the time comes!"

"In the poorhouse, most likely! A fig for your high and mighty ideas about nobility! A business career, that's where the money is! I say, apprentice him to a merchant!"

Vincenzio and Galileo would look at each other and sigh. The best thing to do when Mother was in this mood was to get away as quickly as possible. Away they would hurry, stopping only to take up their lutes, out of the house and down the street, past the great walls of the city, out into the fields. There, in harmony with the birds, Galileo and his father would play and sing together for the rest of the day.

Little by little, Galileo began to meet boys his own age. One lad, Rica Baroni, son of a wealthy patrician, became his best friend. They spent hours talking about their dreams and ambitions. Galileo was interested mostly in reading books. But Rica dreamed only of travel to faraway places and dangerous, exciting adventures. Often, they were joined by a neighbor, a fat boy named Niccolo Riccardi, who ardently desired to become a priest. In the company of his friends, Galileo forgot his loneliness.

One day, Vincenzio told Galileo, "I am planning to write a book."

"A book? You, Father? How splendid! You will be famous, and I shall tell everyone, 'I am Galileo, son of the famous author Vincenzio Galilei!'"

Vincenzio tousled Galileo's hair good-naturedly. "I am afraid your imagination is a little too great, my son. I shall not be famous. But perhaps my book will be useful. I am going to compare ancient methods of composing music with modern styles."

He told Galileo how he planned to show that some of the older and more venerated authorities on music had been wrong about certain things.

"But, Father, isn't it wrong to say such things about famous people? If everyone thinks these authorities were right, how can you say they were not?"

"I see it is time to make some things about life clearer to you," sighed Vincenzio. "Listen carefully, for what I have to say may be very important to you some day."

Galileo sat, chin on fist, legs drawn up, a fierce little bundle of concentration.

"You will find in this world, Galileo, many, many people—perhaps far too many—who are always willing to take someone else's word for the truth. They are always ready to say something is true because so-and-so said it, or because they read it in such-and-such a book. This is the easy way of getting along, the way of people who are afraid of change, afraid of new ideas. This way, you must never, never be.

"Do not be afraid to challenge authority at any time, if a search for truth is in question. Truth is not found behind a man's reputation. Truth appears only through the search for the answers to questions by a free mind. Whatever you do, never accept mere authority as proof that something is right or wrong. This is not the easy path in life, but it is the most rewarding.

"Well, that was quite a sermon! I did not mean to make a long-winded speech." Vincenzio held out his hand. "Let's have a try at that new piece for the organ I composed yesterday."

Galileo leaped to his feet. His serious eyes looked full into his father's face. "I'll remember what you said, Father." Vincenzio laid his arm lovingly about the boy's shoulders, and they went into the music room.

The summer came, and with it a new danger—the plague. Every summer, the noble families of Florence moved out of the city into villas in the country to avoid the pestilence that seemed to come with the first hot days. Many of the people who remained in the city grew ill and died. First only a few died, then more and more. The church bells tolled all day for the dead. Carts loaded with bodies rattled through the streets at night, bound for the great burying pits outside the city walls. People feared to leave their houses. Shops closed, and there was little meat or bread to be had.

Over all of Florence hung the smell of the plague. Galileo and his sister and brother could no longer leave the house. From the window, Galileo could see an occasional doctor go by, wearing the usual plague costume, a dark heavy cloak that covered the entire figure and a mask that held a sponge filled with aromatic vinegar to the nose. The smell of vinegar was thought to be a sure method of keeping the disease away.

Vincenzio returned from the court in a state of great excitement. "Pack up!" he shouted to his wife. "We're getting out of here. The Duke has given his consent for us to accompany him to his villa in the mountains for the rest of the summer. We can get out of this forsaken city of death!"

He turned to Galileo. "And I have special news for you, son. The monks at Vallombrosa have consented to accept you as a pupil in their advanced school at the monastery. There you will not only be safe from the plague, but you will further your education as befits a noble person."

Galileo didn't know whether to be sad because he couldn't go with the Duke to the mountains—that sounded exciting—or to be happy because he was getting a chance to learn more. Being with the court in the summer lodge was probably fun. Galileo thought of the handsome bearded courtiers striding about, heads high, with their long sword scabbards slapping against their thighs. There would be hunting with falcons in the meadows. The beaters would move in the forest, driving the wild boars from the underbrush.

Then he thought about books, especially the new ones he would have a chance to read at the monastery of Vallombrosa. That, he decided, was far more exciting. Michelangelo and his mother might think that was a queer way to feel, but Galileo loved books and reading. Just thinking about going back to school, he became terribly excited. He grasped his father's hand.

"What is it like there? Do they have many books? Will I learn more mathematics? Do they—"

"Whoa, whoa, there, little stallion! Don't get into such a fever—there's enough fever in Florence already! Vallombrosa is a lovely spot; they have many books. Perhaps they will also teach mathematics. Time enough to find out when you get there. And now, everybody, on with the packing!"

Vallombrosa, Galileo found, was just what the name meant—the shady valley. Here, a few miles out of Florence, the city no longer existed. Instead, there were beautiful hills, dark green with trees, meadows full of grasses and white and yellow wild flowers, and, centered among them, the monastery. The buildings were of stone, with slate roofs. There was a bell tower that reached up into the sky, far above the rest of the monastery.

When Galileo came, the place was so quiet, it seemed like the end of the world. The creaking and rattling of the cart in which he rode seemed strange and unnatural. Galileo went through the gate and up to the great center door. He grasped the big iron knocker firmly and rapped twice. He could hear the thud booming through the silent halls of the monastery; all was quiet again.

Then, there was the long squeak of a bolt being drawn back. A man's voice asked, "Who's there?"

"I am Galileo Galilei, son of Vincenzio Galilei of Florence."

The huge door of the monastery opened with a slight creaking sound. A hand reached out to take his arm gently. "Come in, come in, and welcome, Galileo Galilei. Forgive my questioning you before I opened the door, but these are times when it is best not to open doors to any passer-by."

Galileo blinked. Coming from the bright sun into the cool gloom of the monastery corridor, it was difficult to see for a moment. Then, the blurry figure before him focused into an elderly man, dressed in a long brownish robe belted with a rough piece of rope. On his shoulders, the robe ended in a great cowl that could cover his head, which was quite bald and shiny.

"I am Father Paulus. Come, I will show you where you will sleep. But one moment, let me ask you if you feel well. Do you feel hot or dizzy? Do your eyes hurt? Any ache in your shoulders or neck?"

"Why, no," said Galileo, a little bewildered.

"Don't be alarmed. It's only to make sure that you have not brought the plague with you from the city. Come along now to the dormitory."

The dormitory was a long room with many beds and windows. Father Paulus pointed to one of the beds. On it was a long sack filled with straw for a mattress. There was a small bench at the foot of the bed and, at the head, a little crudely made table. "You'll find life is very simple here, Galileo. We eat and drink good food to keep us strong. We sleep eight hours each night so that we may have our wits about us during the day. We work for the glory of God and for the good of men. But, most of all, we revere learning. If you want to learn, as your father says you do, then we bid you welcome."

Soon, Galileo settled down to the routine life of the monastery of Vallombrosa. There were about fifty boys at the school, from youngsters like his brother Michelangelo to boys of twelve, his own age. The monks who taught and regulated the lives of the boys were kind and gentle, but very strict. Every day was like the one before it. Rise at five o'clock. Half an hour to wash and tidy one's quarters. Then morning prayers. Breakfast at six-thirty. First lessons at seven o'clock. Noon prayers at twelve. Lunch at half past. Siesta, or rest period, until two. Afternoon lessons until five. Evening prayers and supper. Study hours until nine. Then, lights out and to bed.

Galileo found the life monotonous, but pleasant. He grew very fond of some of his teachers, especially of Father Paulus, who taught him Latin literature. Now Galileo could read the most difficult Latin books with ease. In fact, he learned to write Latin as easily as the language he spoke at home. Swelling with pride, he wrote his first all-Latin letter home to his father: *Ave, Optimus et Nobilissimus Pater!*

To his regret, none of the monks was skilled in mathematics. In fact, most were amazed to learn the Pythagorean number games he had learned in the house of Master Jacopo Borghini. Yet, in some of the lessons in logic, which was the study of argument, Galileo found ideas which were rather exciting. He learned that a man named Aristotle had written many, many years before about such things as falling stones, the flight of arrows, and the motion of the stars.

Galileo's ability to read Greek had improved enough for him to read Aristotle's work without much trouble. One day, he sought out Father Paulus.

"Is this true, what Aristotle says here in his book called *Physica?*"

"What is that, Galileo?"

"He says that all earthly matter falls to the ground because it wishes to return to its natural resting place. That is why stones fall down when they are dropped. Is that true?"

"If it is written so in Aristotle, my son, then it must be true."

"It says here also that a heavy stone will fall to earth faster than a light one, since it will rush to its natural place much faster. Is that also true?"

"I know little of such things, Galileo. But if it is written so in Aristotle, then it must be true."

Father Paulus saw the disappointment in Galileo's face. "Come, come, lad, why is this so important?"

"I don't know. I would like to know more about this, Father."

"Well, it's too bad we have no natural philosophers or mathematicians here at Vallombrosa. But at the university in Pisa you would soon find some professor to explain it to you."

The university! That was where you went to study to be a doctor or a lawyer. Galileo had heard his father speak of the great university of Pisa. But Galileo also knew one important fact about the university. It took a great deal of money to go there. And money was one thing that the noble family of Galilei lacked.

At Vallombrosa, the years passed so quickly that Galileo scarcely noticed. He had been twelve years old on that hot day when he had left the plague-filled city of Florence for the shady valley. Now, suddenly, he was no longer a boy, but a young man of fifteen.

Galileo became accustomed to the calm and orderly life. Gradually, he began to feel sympathetic toward the ways of the monks, their relaxed and simple ways, and their devotion to learning. One day, he wrote a letter home and told his father he was thinking of joining the order of monks at Vallombrosa.

The letter brought an excited Vincenzio, tired and dusty from his quick ride, to the monastery.

"Is this true, what you write here?"

"Is it wrong to want to be a monk, Father?"

"No, it's not wrong. But it's not what I want for you, Galileo. I had thought your life would be concerned with other things."

"A merchant's apprentice, perhaps?"

"Don't look down upon merchants, son. Their money makes them powerful men." After a hasty glance at Galileo's face, Vincenzio said, "Well, I had thought of the university—"

"The university!" Galileo's bitter mood vanished. He grew excited and waved his arms about. "Can I go there? Do you have the money? Father Paulus said I could learn more about mathematics and philosophy there. And astronomy, too! When can I go? When—"

"Whoa, whoa!" cried Vincenzio. "There you go again, rearing on your hind legs like a horse with a thistle under the saddle! I said, I had thought of the university—"

"Please, Father. I want to go to the university more than anything else in the world."

"Well, we shall see. The first thing is to get you out of here."

"Father Paulus will be disappointed to know I am leaving."

Vincenzio stroked his short pointed beard.

"You cannot remain here and attend the university at the same time. Which do you choose?"

"What a question, Father! The university, of course. It's just that I don't want to hurt Father Paulus. He has been a good friend to me."

"Besides," said Vincenzio, "in your last few letters, you have complained that your eyes have been hurting. I am sure it comes from squinting at all those books. I will tell Father Paulus that I am taking you home to Florence to have a physician look at your eyes."

Galileo sighed. "Very well, Father. Yet, I do hate to leave Vallombrosa. It's so peaceful here, and I have been happy. Still, if it means going to the university—"

"I have another splendid idea!" exclaimed Vincenzio. "I'll write a letter to the Grand Duke petitioning for a scholarship for you. There are forty free places in the university for poor scholars. I am sure you can get one."

Heart beating wildly at the thought of the new adventure to come, Galileo prepared to leave Vallombrosa.

After the first full week of gladness to be home, Galileo began to find life intolerable. His mother nagged him until he was miserable. Michelangelo, whom she favored, took advantage of his big brother's return to avoid all the unpleasant duties he had been performing in the house. Galileo found himself caring for Virginia, washing the dishes, and mopping the floors.

Whenever he tried to escape some unpleasant task, Madam Giulia would scream at him, "Well, if you don't want to earn your keep by honest work around the house, why don't you find a paying job? A fellow your size, fifteen years old, doesn't exactly eat like a bird! A nobleman, indeed! Better get rid of those fancy ideas your father put into your head about the university. Oh, yes, I know all about that!"

"I shall go to the university, Mother!"

"You'll go as easily as I can fly right up this chimney! Better think seriously about something more practical. Yesterday, I was talking to the secretary of Marco Pontelli, the wool merchant. Now, he said if you were to—"

But whenever Madam Giulia began to talk of his becoming an apprentice, Galileo would cover his ears and run from the room.

It was winter again. Galileo was sixteen years old. He began to read seriously now. There was a new book he had found, written by one of the ancient Greeks named Euclid. It was about something called geometry—that meant *earth-measuring*. Geometry was a kind of mathematical game played with lines, triangles, and circles; but Galileo did not quite understand how the game was played.

And he learned something new—how to paint in oil colors, His father asked one of the court artists to give Galileo lessons. The man soon saw that Galileo had talent and encouraged him to think about choosing painting as a career.

When he was not working in the house, painting, or playing the lute, Galileo would sit by the hour and write poetry. The monks at Vallombrosa were men with good literary taste. With them, Galileo had read the works of many famous poets. So, it was not difficult for him to write good poetry himself.

Vincenzio was proud and happy that his son could read Greek and Latin with ease, that he could paint and write poetry so well, and that he could play the lute and the viola. The ability to do these things well was the mark of a noble person.

Madam Giulia, on the other hand, thought little of such accomplishments. "So he can smear paints with a brush! So he can dirty a piece of paper with ink! So he can twang away like a lazybones on that lute of his for hours! How is he going to make a living?"

Vincenzio kept his mouth shut. By now, he knew that to argue with his wife was useless.

One day, Galileo met his father at the door. It had been snowing hard all day. Vincenzio shook the white snow from his heavy cape. Then he held his cold hands over the fire and chafed them.

"A bitter day, even for dogs!"

"Father, has there been any word from the Grand Duke?"

Vincenzio scowled into the fire. Then he turned toward Galileo with solemn face. "You might as well know now as later. Your scholarship was refused. No reason. There's nothing to do, but to apply again next year."

"Next year? But at Vallombrosa you promised!"

"I didn't know, lad. I didn't expect this to happen. And, to tell you the truth, I thought there might be a chance to borrow the money. But the chance didn't turn up—"

Galileo was terribly disappointed. If he had been spoiled, like his brother Michelangelo, he would probably have thrown himself down on the floor in a tantrum. But he was a Galilei, a noble youth, and his father's son. He bit his lip hard for a moment, and then shrugged his shoulders.

"Well, what can't be helped can't be helped!"

Vincenzio embraced his son with one arm. "Think about it, my boy. After all, Marco Pontelli doesn't lead a bad life, even if he is rather stuffy and pompous. He strolls about in black velvet robes, finer than those of a professor. He lives in a palace, and has many servants to wait upon him hand and foot. And he began life as an apprentice to a wool merchant."

"I don't know why, Father, but I would rather have a hundred books than a thousand florins. I guess I don't care very much about being rich. I'd rather be wise and happy, like you."

Vincenzio hugged his son. Tears sprang into his eyes. "Thank you, son. I would rather hear you say that than have a thousand florins, too." He stepped back, face serious again. "But, there's your mother to consider, and your brother and sister."

"What do you mean?"

"What if I were to die?" As Galileo started, Vincenzio put out a hand. "No, don't speak—one must always be aware of such possibilities. There is little money to take care of them. This is why I would ask you to think about becoming an apprentice."

"I'll think about it, Father." Galileo moved toward his room and then turned. "But I'll think about the university, too."

That night, Galileo could not sleep. He tossed and turned, thinking about what to do. The chances of attending the university were smaller than ever. Good-by, mathematics and astronomy! Good-by, books and learning! My family comes first, he said to himself. With a cold chill, he remembered his father's words: *What if I were to die?* Galileo knew what he had to do.

In the morning, he came to the breakfast table white-faced and tired from lack of sleep.

"That's what you get from staying up and reading those books all night!" scolded his mother. "Never mind the cost of using extra candles!"

Galileo smiled, in spite of the annoyance he felt. His mother would never change. "No, I did not read last night. But I did think a great deal. And I'm willing to work for Pontelli, the wool merchant, if you can arrange it."

Madam Giulia clapped her hands to her head. "Am I hearing things?" she cried. "The boy has finally come to his senses!"

Galileo turned toward his father, looking for the approval he expected to see in Vincenzio's face. But Vincenzio had risen from his chair, and his face was set and determined. He crashed his fist among the dishes.

"No! By the powers above, I say no! I, too, have been thinking all night. If Galileo wants to go to the university, he shall go!"

He turned to Madam Giulia. The look of happiness had vanished from her face. "I know what you are thinking, my love, But tell me this, what other profession in Florence, nay, in all Italy, does as well as Pontelli's, but has social prestige as well, eh?"

Madam Giulia was speechless.

"What about a physician?"

"A physician? I hadn't thought—"

"That's because you know nothing of the Galilei family, my dear. My ancestor, after whom Galileo was named, was professor of medicine at the University of Florence about a hundred and fifty years ago. And he was an important man in the city government, too! Why shouldn't Galileo study medicine?"

"But, the money——"

"I have thought about it. I had forgotten all about a little bonus of fifty florins promised to me by the Duke some time ago. If I remind him gently, I know he'll pay me without delay. That money will pay at least for Galileo's first year. We'll worry about the rest later."

"It costs money to live in Pisa."

"You forget our kinsman, Muzio Tedaldi, my dear. He will be glad to take Galileo into his house, I am sure."

Vincenzio clapped the astounded Galileo on the back. "Well, then, it's settled! I'll arrange for you to begin in the September session at the Medical School."

Galileo felt as though the top of his head would fly off right up through the ceiling and into the sky. He wanted to hug and kiss his parents and Michelangelo and Virginia, and to cry and laugh and sing all at once.

Instead, he sank back into his chair and stared straight ahead. In only six months, he would be at Pisa. In September, Galileo Galilei would be wearing the long black gown of the university student. The world of wonder and learning was waiting for him.

Chapter III

Galileo became accustomed to many new ways at the University of Pisa.

Every day he would put on, over his regular clothes, the long black gown that marked him as a student. On his head, he wore a black cap with a flat top. At the university, great respect was shown for the teachers. Whenever Galileo passed one of the professors, he had to nod and take off his hat. The Grand Duke's fifty florins had changed Galileo's world, indeed.

On special occasions, which occurred about once a month, there was an academic procession. Sometimes the procession marched to the great lecture hall for the awarding of a doctor's degree to a successful candidate. At other times, there was a procession to the chapel, or perhaps to the outdoor arena, where disputations were heard.

"Well, Galileo, tell me about the university. Are you enjoying it as much as you expected?"

It was Muzio, Galileo's uncle, who spoke. They were both sitting by the hearth in Muzio's small but snug house, warming their hands at the fire. Opposite them. Madam Tedaldi sat hunched over a pair of hose she was patching.

"I am very happy there, Uncle."

"Tell me about the university. What do you like best?"

Galileo smiled. "Well, that's hard to say. I love to watch the academic processions."

"Academic processions? Ah, yes, I've heard about them. But I've never had a chance to see one. What's it like?"

Galileo arose from his chair and began to describe the procession for his uncle. As he spoke, he strode up and down the room, imitating the various members of the faculty.

"It's very grand! First comes the Chancellor in his round red cap and his velvet gown trimmed with fur. His stomach sticks out so, and he waddles a bit. He carries the staff of authority in his right hand, as though he were ready to give a beating to anyone who dared smile."

Muzio roared with laughter at Galileo's imitation of the Chancellor. His wife, astonished, stopped sewing to watch.

"Now comes the Dean. He, too, has a red gown, though it is not as grand as the Chancellor's. The Dean is getting old. It's a long walk for him now. He leans on his staff like this, but in a very dignified manner." And Galileo hobbled across the room.

"After the Dean comes the Rector. He hands out awards and punishments, you know, and hasn't a friend in the university. So he has to walk very haughtily. His nose is up in the air, as though he were saying, 'I don't give a fig for your opinions; I am an important man, and I know it!'"

Tedaldi and his wife were howling with laughter and holding their stomachs.

"Now come the noble professors. First the doctors, with their very fancy gowns trimmed with black velvet hangings, and their hoods of all colors. Their wisdom hangs heavy on their heads." Galileo scrunched up his head, as though a heavy iron weight were resting on it.

"Then follow the masters. They stagger a little, because they are still dizzy from studying for the doctor's degree. Finally, here come the bachelors. That doesn't mean that they have no wives, you know. It means that they are not yet married to wisdom." That was an old university joke, but Muzio and his wife enjoyed it as though it had just fallen from the lips of the latest favorite stage comedian.

"Oh, that was rich!" exclaimed Muzio, clutching his sides. "I am weak, I shall perish! Who needs to go to the comic opera? All one needs is a Galileo in the house! Tell us more about the university."

"Then, there are the disputations."

"What in the name of seven tinkers are dis—pu—pu—tations?" It was a difficult word for Muzio to pronounce.

"All candidates for all degrees must argue a thesis against all comers in the disputation arena. For example, suppose I am to become a bachelor in medicine. I choose a thesis. Title: 'The Humors of the Spleen Are More Inflamed During Months Which Have the Letter S.' On a certain day, all who wish to dispute this statement come to the arena to challenge me."

"What happens then?"

"Why, then some old physician with a long beard and a nose grown red from smelling too much vinegar asks, 'Who is your authority for this thesis?' And I say boldly, 'It is so written by the great master physician Dr. Muzio Tedaldi, on page fourteen, line one, of his famous volume *On Humors*

of the Spleen in Goats, based reliably on the work of the noted ancient physician N.P.L.!'"

"N.P.L.? What does that stand for?"

"No patients living!"

Again, the little room resounded with laughter. Strangely enough, Galileo talked in this funny and sarcastic fashion about medicine all the time. He was not able to take his medical studies very seriously.

There were some things he did not talk about in the Tedaldi home. He did not tell them that he often neglected his medical lectures to attend lectures on philosophy and science. And he did not tell about the disputation he had attended a few days before.

The defender of the thesis had been a candidate for the bachelor's degree in natural science. The thesis had been "Of Two Earthly Bodies That Fall to the Ground from the Same Height, the Heavier Shall Outrun the Lighter in Proportion to Their Weights." At first, the authority for this statement had been questioned, although everyone knew it was Aristotle.

"The body with more earth in its composition," said the candidate, "will surely rush toward its natural resting place more quickly and will therefore strike the ground first. In fact, the speeds of falling are in proportion to the weights of the bodies. It is written in Aristotle that a stone weighing ten times more than another will fall ten times as fast."

Galileo could not contain himself. "Have you ever tried the experiment to see if it really happens that way?"

There was a hush. Apparently, this was the wrong kind of question to ask. It was shocking for a freshman to ask any questions at all at a dispute.

The candidate squinted to see who had spoken. "Aha!" he cried. "It is a fledgling who speaks!" Philosophy and science students usually made fun of the medical students, and all three looked down their noses at the law students. "What need is there for such nonsense, when it is written so in black and white in Aristotle?"

Galileo shouted even louder. "What proof is there that Aristotle ever tried the experiment?"

An angry buzzing swept over the crowd of professors and students. For most of them, the word of Aristotle was like the word of God, never to be doubted.

"Well," laughed the candidate, "our little medicine-mixer would wrangle with anyone, even Aristotle himself. Have you ever tried the experiment, wrangler?"

There were shouts from the crowd. "Answer him! Speak up, wrangler! Fight! Fight! Shame! Shame!"

Angry and red-faced, Galileo elbowed his way out of the crowd. In a moment, his questions had been forgotten, and a new disputation begun. But the nickname had stuck; now all his classmates called him the Wrangler.

One morning, a few months later, as Galileo left the medical lecture hall, he was stopped by a short, mustached man, dressed in the fancy hose and robe usually seen at the court in Florence.

"Your pardon, young man, aren't you Galileo, son of Vincenzio Galilei of Florence?"

"Why, yes."

"I am a good friend of your father, and I bring you greetings from him."

"Is he well?"

"His health is good, and the work on his book is progressing steadily."

It made Galileo very happy to hear about his father. Then he remembered his manners. "I thank you, good sir, for your news. And whom do I have the honor of addressing?"

"I am Ostilio Ricci, tutor in mathematics to the pages of the Grand Duke. He has just arrived in Pisa to spend the remainder of the winter and the spring. I took the first opportunity to come and bring word from your father."

"You really teach mathematics? Do you know anything about Euclid's geometry?"

Ricci smiled. "I expect so. As a matter of fact, I'm giving a geometry lesson to the pages this very afternoon."

"Signor Ricci, I have a great favor to ask."

"Well, what is it?" Is he going to borrow money already, on such short acquaintance? thought Ricci. He understood the major problem of university students only too well.

"I want to attend your geometry classes."

"Why, I thought you were a medical student."

"So I am. But that is because my father wishes it. He says that medicine is the best-paying profession."

"He's not wrong."

"I'd rather study mathematics and astronomy."

"But, Galileo, you have only to compare the yearly salaries of the professor of medicine here at the university—two thousand florins!—with that of the highest-paid mathematics professor—about sixty florins! Mathematics pays poorly."

"I don't care about money. I love mathematics best. Will you help me?"

Ricci began to question Galileo's understanding of mathematics. As Galileo replied, the tutor's amazement grew. Here was a boy with a natural talent in mathematics!

At last, Ricci said, "You have acquired a great store of mathematical knowledge, indeed. How old are you?"

"Seventeen."

"This needs looking into. When I return to Florence, I will speak seriously to your father about this matter. To waste such a talent upon medicine! Meanwhile, you may come to my geometry classes. Come today, if you have no lectures."

Galileo was so happy, he could not speak. He wrung Signor Ricci's hand in gratitude.

"You have a strong grip, I see. Enough, leave a few fingers unbroken. At the Grand Duke's palace, then, at three. You know where it is? Good. I will leave word with the guard at the gates."

As the tutor walked away, a group of fellow students, looking like black crows in their gowns, approached.

"Look, boys, it's the Wrangler!"

"Give us an argument, Wrangler!"

"What are you disputing today, Wrangler?"

"Up with Aristotle! Down with the Wrangler!"

Ordinarily, such banter would have enraged Galileo. At this moment, however, he only smiled sweetly at the students, stretched out his arms, and cried, "Today, I love you all like brothers!"

The students looked at one another in amazement. One made a motion with his fingers against the side of his head. "Poor Galileo! He's finally gone mad! Too much wrangling!"

Galileo, lost in dreams of the new knowledge he was soon to gain, had already forgotten they were there.

Under Ostilio Ricci's guidance, Galileo became familiar with Euclidian geometry. There were the rules of the game to learn, then theorems about lines, triangles, circles, and rectangles. Galileo swallowed up geometry so rapidly that Signor Ricci predicted, "Soon you will teach me about geometry."

One afternoon, Galileo arrived at the Grand Duke's palace boiling over with excitement.

"Well, what now?" Ricci was quite used to Galileo's becoming wildly excited about anything mathematical.

"Signor Ricci! Signor Ricci! I—I—" Galileo was all out of breath.

"Take it easy, boy, take it easy! There's nothing so important that you have to turn purple in the face about it!"

Galileo drew in a big breath and blew it out with a great sigh. "This is important, sir. I have made a discovery—I think it's an important one—I don't think anyone else knows about it—"

"Come, come! Don't jabber like an ape! Make sense! Just what have you discovered?"

"It's about the swinging of a pendulum, sir! The length of the pendulum alone determines the time of the swing!"

"What on earth—?"

"Let me show you. I brought it with me." Galileo drew a length of string from his pocket. At one end of the string was tied his house key. "Here is a ready-made pendulum. The key is the pendulum bob. Now I hold it by the other end and let the key swing freely. Supposing we count the time it takes to make one whole swing."

"That's not a very easy thing to do."

"But I can show you how. Just use your pulse. It beats regularly, and so marks off fairly equal intervals of time."

"You are right! It takes a doctor to think of that!" Ricci found the pulse of his left wrist with the fingers of his right hand. "Ready. Let it swing."

The key curved down and then flashed upwards again. "Three pulse beats and a part."

"That was for a full swing," said Galileo. "Now let the pendulum swing awhile. What happens to the path of the swing?"

"Why, it gets shorter and shorter, until the pendulum stops swinging. That's common knowledge."

"Ah, yes. But this isn't. There, now, the pendulum has slowed down. The path is about half as long as it was before. Now, count again."

Ricci felt his wrist and counted. "By—! Why—! Three pulse beats and a part! Exactly the same time as before! It's impossible!"

"It's the truth! For a pendulum this long, all the swings take exactly three beats and a part! Now, observe, I shorten the string. What happens?"

"The pendulum swings faster."

"Exactly. But each swing still takes precisely as much time as the one before!"

"This is an amazing discovery, indeed! How did you happen to think of it?"

"I was sitting in the cathedral this morning. I often go there to think out things. It's so cool and quiet. There aren't many people there in the morning. Well, this morning, one of the warders lit an oil lamp that was hanging on the wall from a chain. When he let it go, it began to swing—a pendulum, you see? And suddenly, I had a wild thought about timing the swings! I don't know where it came from. But I didn't have any kind of clock with me. Lord knows, whatever kinds of clocks we have today are pretty useless anyway. So I thought for a moment—and then it came to me! The human heart is a clock. It beats regularly most of the time, except when one is ill or under a strain. Then, it was natural to think of using the pulse."

"Well, this is rather staggering. I must sit down." Ricci plumped himself down on a velvet-covered chair. "First we must think about the usefulness of this discovery."

"I have already thought of one use."

Ricci shook his head. "I should have expected that of you. Well, what can you do with this strange property of the pendulum?"

"Use it just in reverse."

"And just what does that mean?"

"When a doctor comes to treat an illness, what is his first move? I am enough of a medical student to know the answer to that. He takes the patient's pulse! How do you tell a normal pulse from a sick one? By the variation in pulse beats. A sick person's pulse beats faster or slower than a *normal* pulse.

Now, why can't the pendulum be used to count pulse beats very exactly?"

"Why not, indeed!"

"I have already thought of an invention for this purpose. Look, supposing I have a stick of a certain length. From a nail at the top I hang a string, just a bit shorter than the stick, and tie a little metal ball at the end. Now I have a pendulum of fixed length. I take a pulse I consider to be normal. I can wind the string about the nail until the pendulum is just the right length. The time between each pulse beat is exactly the same as the time for each full swing of the pendulum. I mark the length of this pendulum on the wood—and this mark means a normal pulse!"

Ricci jumped up. "And if the time between pulse beats is less than the time for the pendulum swing, the pendulum has to be shortened further, in order to equalize the times. This indicates a fast pulse. Why, this is wonderful! This is sheer genius!"

Galileo was pleased at the compliment. "I have decided upon a name for this instrument. It will be called the Pulsilogia."

"Come, we must not lose a moment!" Ricci took Galileo by the hand. "We must search out the court physician and tell him of your marvelous invention! You have made a good start toward being a doctor already, Galileo! The Pulsilogia will allow a physician to detect even the slightest abnormality in the beating of a pulse!"

Galileo hung back. "But that's just it, Signor Ricci. I don't want to be a doctor. I want to be a mathematician!"

Ricci threw up his hands in mock horror. "Forgive me! I almost forgot! This business with the pendulum knocked it out of my head! How stupid of me! But I have been to Florence and have spoken with your father."

"Did he give his consent? What did he say?"

"He has consented!"

Galileo was about to whoop for joy. Ricci put a hand over his mouth. "Quiet, for heaven's sake! This is the Duke's palace, not a wineshop! But there is a condition."

"A condition?"

"Yes, you may study mathematics and astronomy. But only on condition that you continue your medical studies."

Galileo's face fell. "But I thought—"

"Why such a sour face? Come, the bargain is not so bad. At least, part of the battle is won. Perhaps when I tell him of the Pulsilogia, we will win the rest. Come now, let's find the court physician!"

A month later, Galileo received a letter from Florence. It was in his father's handwriting. Galileo tore the envelope open eagerly; he missed Vincenzio very much.

> *Greetings, my dear son:*
>
> *All is well here with us. Michelangelo is studying music with me, and shows himself quite proficient. Virginia is getting to be quite the young lady, and is already talking of suitors! Ricci has written about your fabulous invention. You can't imagine how proud and happy I am! Indeed, the court physician has already spread the news of the Pulsilogia all over Florence. The name of Galileo is on everyone's lips.*
>
> *This brings me to the matter in hand. In light of what*

Ricci has told me, I have reconsidered my insistence on your becoming a physician. If mathematics is the career for which the Lord has suited you, then, mathematics it is! I will not stand in your way. May all good fortune be yours!

Your loving father,
Vincenzio Galilei

P.S. *The family all send their love. Even Mother is quite overwhelmed by the success of your invention!*

Galileo's heart was bursting with happiness. Now the world was to be his! He ran to the administration office of the university to make the necessary changes in his program. What good fortune! Instead of those uninteresting lectures on medicinal plants and pharmacy, he would listen to lectures on the real miracles of nature—the sun, the planets, the stars!

I have everything in life I want now, thought Galileo; I shall never have another worry in the world.

Now the days and the months began to fly like the wind. Galileo did not miss a lecture on astronomy or mathematics. It was not like the early days, when he had gone to the lectures halfheartedly, and had sat there dreaming of geometry problems.

His Uncle Muzio, though a simple worker, showed an interest in Galileo's studies. He was forever asking Galileo to explain the lectures of the professors. At first, Galileo was somewhat irritated by Muzio's questioning. What was the purpose of explaining this complicated knowledge to a curious old man? After a while, he realized that in explaining the principles of astronomy and mathematics to Muzio, he understood them better himself.

"Now, tell me, Galileo, what is all this purpose of astronomy? Is it to tell man's fate in this world?"

Galileo smiled. "No, no, Uncle! You are thinking of astrology. That is another matter—the telling of fortunes by the stars. I am not sure I believe in that very much. An astronomer's task is entirely different. He is interested in the motions of the stars and the planets alone. The astronomer spends his time trying to predict the motion of the heavenly bodies."

"Ah, yes, I have heard about that. Your old Muzio is not as ignorant as you think. It concerns a man named Ptolemy, isn't that so?"

"You're right, Uncle! Claudius Ptolemy was the Greek mathematician who lived in the city of Alexandria in ancient Egypt—about thirteen hundred years ago." Galileo told Muzio how Ptolemy had perfected the world system of Aristotle. The earth was the great important place in the world, placed there by the Creator for man to inhabit.

The great earth sat motionless in the center of the world. On the earth, nothing was perfect or permanent—everything kept changing. Leaves on the trees grew brown and fell, wood burned and changed to gray ash, men were born and died. But the heavenly bodies which moved in the sky about the earth were perfect—they never changed. The moon and the sun appeared smooth and round and perfect. They moved about the earth in the most perfect geometrical path—a circle.

"What is perfect about a circle?"

"Don't you see, Uncle, every part of a circle is the same distance from the center. Think of a cartwheel. All the spokes are the same length. That is a kind of perfection."

Galileo explained more about the world system of Ptolemy and Aristotle. About the earth, the heavenly bodies were ranged in this order: first the moon, then the planets Mercury and Venus, and then the sun. The outermost planets were Mars, Jupiter, and Saturn. Out beyond Saturn, the great circle of fixed stars, the constellations, turned about the earth once a day, as did the circle of the sun. Thus, night and day could be explained. If one used geometry properly, then the future positions of the planets could be predicted.

"What's out there beyond the stars?" asked Muzio.

Galileo turned his hands palms up. "Who knows? Man cannot see that far with his eyes. Ptolemy considers that to be the realm of God, the Prime Mover of the world."

Muzio was properly impressed. "All that seems a very difficult business, indeed."

Galileo sighed. "Sometimes, I think it is too difficult to be correct. It seems to me that nature was intended to be explained in simple and beautiful mathematical terms."

Galileo heard, too, of a new system of the world, fashioned by a man who had died only about forty years before—a Polish astronomer and mathematician named Copernicus. In this system, the sun was considered to be the center of the world, while the earth took its place among the planets which moved about the sun. The astronomers at Pisa thought that the ideas of Copernicus were ridiculous.

One day, Galileo stopped the chief professor of astronomy in the great entrance hall of the university. The white-haired astronomer, stooped over in his heavy velvet robe, listened patiently while Galileo asked his question.

"Sir, why is it not possible to consider that the earth moves about the sun, as Copernicus has said?"

"This motion of the earth going about the sun is just some Pythagorean nonsense this Copernicus picked up when he studied here in Italy! In the first place, why do we not feel this earthly motion? In the second place, in order to explain the occurrence of day and night, Copernicus has the earth rotating on its axis. This is sheer foolishness!"

"Why so?"

"Why, if the earth turned, then a great wind would be blowing continuously! Everything on the earth's surface would be swept away. But the houses stand! The trees stand! And the birds—why doesn't the earth turn under them while they are in the air? Believe me, young man, Aristotle and Ptolemy are not to be doubted on this matter. Our eyes, our senses of motion, everything in the name of common sense tells us that the earth is motionless, and that the sun moves about it."

"But isn't it true that by the system of Copernicus, the position of Mars can be predicted by simpler mathematics?"

The professor sighed. "Well, so I have heard. Anyway, his simple mathematics is so confoundedly difficult, I can hardly understand it. It's just some kind of trick he invented. It is all right to play with Copernican mathematics as an exercise. But never forget for a moment that the world of Ptolemy is the true world!"

"But in Pythagoras, mathematics and nature are inseparable—"

The professor leaned toward Galileo and peered at him with near-sighted eyes. "Eh? Aren't you the one they call the Wrangler? Aren't you Galileo?"

"Yes, sir."

"Hmm, I should have known! My advice to you, young man, is to forget Pythagoras, and to concentrate on Aristotle. And now I have some work to do."

Galileo was dismissed. He stood for a moment, angry and dismayed. Then he remembered what his father had once said. "Do not be afraid to challenge authority at any time, if a search for truth is in question. This is not the easy path in life, but it is the most rewarding."

I shall discover the truth, thought Galileo, and not in any old books. He walked over to a window and stared up at the blue sky. I shall find the truth up there, he said to himself.

Galileo returned to Florence. It was time for Vincenzio to give him the money to pay for his final semester at the university. In the Galilei home, there was the usual commotion. A new baby sister had arrived a few years before. Her name was Livia. Madam Giulia still scolded everyone for getting in her way, and nagged on and on about everyone being too lazy to work. Michelangelo had grown into a handsome, sensitive boy. He was an excellent musician, through Vincenzio's training. But he was spoiled and unruly. He spent money as rapidly as he got it. If he could not have his own way, he had a tantrum, just as he had done when he was a child. Virginia had become a beautiful girl. There was already talk about finding her a husband.

When Galileo asked about the tuition money, Vincenzio stared at the floor for a moment. He looked as though he were going to cry. It was a strange look for a grown man to have on his face. Galileo knew something was wrong.

"There is no money this year?"

"No, there is no money. I am sorry, Galileo. It's just that with Michelangelo and Virginia growing up, and the baby coming, somehow—"

"It's all right. I understand, Father."

"You don't hate me?"

"Don't be foolish, Father. It's not your fault. But what am I to do?"

"I thought, perhaps, that you could apply again for one of the forty free places. After all, you have done well at the university in the past two years."

"Why not?" Galileo ran to the writing desk for pen and paper. "We'll write to the Grand Duke at once!"

Two weeks later, the answer came. Vincenzio came home to find a despondent Galileo hunched in a chair. "The letter—?"

Galileo handed him the envelope with the Grand Duke's seal. "Don't bother reading it. I can tell you in a word what it says. 'No!'"

Vincenzio put his hand soothingly on Galileo's shoulder. "I'm sorry, my son. But why? Why? I don't understand why!"

Galileo shrugged. "I think I know, Father. You see, I'm not too popular with the professors at Pisa. Do you know what my nickname is up there?" He smiled wryly. "They call me the Wrangler. I ask too many questions for which they have no answers."

"Those old—old—" Vincenzio's face flushed red with rage. "What do they think a university is for? Don't they recognize a brilliant student when they see one? I ought to seek an audience with the Grand Duke and tell him how things are at Pisa!"

"Don't, Father. It will only stir up more trouble, and the professors will hate me more than ever. I'll manage something."

"But what will you do? Almost four years wasted! Why, you are twenty-one years old already! And now you will not even receive your bachelor's degree!"

"Never mind, Father. I will find work. And the years have not been wasted—I will study more and read more by myself."

Galileo jumped from his chair and strode to the window that faced in the direction of Pisa. He stared out with concentrated gaze, as though he could actually see the university buildings miles away.

"Just wait, Father. One day, I'll be in that lecture hall at Pisa again. Only this time, I'll be wearing a professor's cap and gown! And those antiquated Aristotle worshipers—they'll eat their own words! You'll see!"

Chapter IV

"Hey, Galileo! Come out! Come out at once!"

Madam Giulia was shouting and knocking at the door of Galileo's room. He stumbled from the bed, rubbing his eyes, and flung the door open.

"What is it, Mother?"

"The son of the Widow Renaldo is here for you. She has a pain. Go attend to her. And don't forget to collect a fee!"

Galileo yawned and began to shrug on his shirt. "Ah, that Widow Renaldo! Her pains are imaginary. She wastes her good money."

"Who cares? If she wants to throw away half a florin to talk about her pains, let her. Thank the Lord, at least you learned enough medicine at the university to bring a few pennies into the house once in a while. Come into the kitchen; I'll give you some breakfast before you go."

Soon Galileo, with a little box of medicinal herbs and powders in his hand, was on his way to the house of the widow. From the day he had left the university he had been helping to support the Galilei household by practicing medicine in the neighborhood. Of course, he was not a graduated and licensed physician. What he was doing was frowned upon by the medical authorities. But the neighbors of the Galilei family kept his comings and goings a fairly close secret. Wisely Galileo refused to treat any serious disorders whose nature he did not understand.

The Widow Renaldo declared she felt better after Galileo had mixed an ill-smelling brew for her to drink. He had discovered almost at once that people felt cheated if the medicine they were given did not have a horrible taste. He collected his half a florin and set out for home. Halfway there, a familiar figure accosted him.

"Ho, there, Wrangler!"

"By all that's wonderful, Signor Ricci! It's really you!"

"Let's not be so formal. After all, we're old friends. Call me Ostilio, please."

"Very well, Ostilio. It's good to see you."

Ricci looked at the box in Galileo's hand. "What have we here? A mathematical physician?"

Galileo's lips twisted in a shamefaced smile. "I've just been trying to help out in the house. Money is so scarce—"

He gave an apologetic wave of the hand.

The mathematician's face showed amazement. "But this is simply ridiculous! You, going to waste as an amateur physician! Why aren't you earning some money with your mathematics?"

Galileo shrugged his shoulders. "How? No one wants to pay to see a theorem of geometry demonstrated."

"That's where you're wrong. As of tomorrow, I can get you at least five pupils who need tutoring in mathematics. And their fathers can afford to pay very handsomely."

"Ostilio! I would be most grateful!" Galileo seized his hand and wrung it.

"Ouch! That grip of yours! Your affection will break my wrist one of these days. Well, let's not talk any more about that—it's settled. Are you doing any studying these days?"

"I have been reading as much of Archimedes as I can lay my hands on."

"Archimedes has always been your favorite, hasn't he?"

"If I can only begin to be a little like the mathematician he was!"

"Perhaps you will be, some day soon." Ostilio clapped Galileo on the shoulder. "I am late for an appointment. Now, look here, no more of this doctoring nonsense, you understand? Meet me tomorrow morning at ten o'clock—no, better still, I'll come by the house for you. It will impress your mother more. Besides, I do want to have a chat with your father. Till tomorrow!"

Galileo watched Ricci's retreating figure until the mathematician turned a corner and was gone. A chance to teach mathematics! And making money doing what he loved! That should please Madam Giulia, at any rate!

On the corner was a large cask filled with rubbish. As he passed, Galileo tossed the medicine box onto the trash heap. Walking toward home, he felt a new freedom.

A year passed. It was a year during which Galileo taught, studied, and worked almost without pause. The extra money he brought into the house pacified Madam Giulia, though she often reminded him of how rich he might have been by this time, had he become a wool merchant.

One evening, Galileo sat with Vincenzio before the fire. Vincenzio spoke. "We don't get to spend as much time together as in the old days, eh, son?"

"I miss the old days, Father." Galileo thought about the times he and Vincenzio had sat together in the fields, playing their lutes and singing.

"Yes, we had fun. Remember how we used to aggravate your mother by howling that French ballad: *L'homme, l'homme, l'homme armé—*"

Galileo suddenly realized that his father's voice had changed. The mellowness had gone out of it. He looked at Vincenzio with sharper scrutiny. The hair that had once been brown and curly was now white. The little dark, pointed beard was whitish too, and a bit scraggly. Vincenzio had grown old.

Galileo showed him a letter, written on very magnificent stationery. "Look, Father, I received this yesterday."

Vincenzio held the letter toward the fire and squinted at the handwriting. "The Marquis del Monte! Oh, I have heard of him. He is a very rich nobleman!"

"And a fine mathematician, too."

Vincenzio read the letter. "He says some very fine things about you here. What is this about a hydro—hydro—what the devil!—hydrostatic balance?"

"That is a set of scales I invented which a goldsmith can use to discover the percentages of each metal in an alloy of silver and gold. Actually, I borrowed the idea from Archimedes."

Vincenzio smiled proudly. "The important thing is that you did something with that idea!" He handed the letter back to Galileo. "This marquis is an important man. His friendship should be valuable."

"I hope so, Father. You see, I have applied for the position of professor of mathematics at the University of Bologna. The professorship is now vacant, and I thought perhaps—"

"I shall use whatever little influence I have to help you," promised Vincenzio.

Galileo's application for the position was rejected. He worked harder than ever at his mathematical studies. More reading of Archimedes inspired him to write an essay about the center of gravity in bodies—the point where the weight of a body is concentrated. He showed this essay to Ricci.

"This is capital! I will have copies of this made at once! All the mathematicians in Italy will want to read this!"

"Do you really think it's good enough?"

"What a foolish question for a modern Archimedes to ask!"

Galileo was filled with joy. He valued the opinion of Ricci very highly. After a few months, he received a letter from Rome. It was from the great astronomer Father Clavius, the scientist who had reformed the calendar at the request of Pope Gregory XIII. Galileo enjoyed his correspondence with fellow mathematicians. They sent each other problems and solutions through the mails. It was a way of conversing pleasantly with many widespread friends.

He wrote the Marquis del Monte:

Your Lordship:

It has come to my ears that the chair of mathematics at Pisa, my old university, is now vacant. This chair, as you probably know, is in the gift of the Grand Duke of Florence. May I take advantage of your friendship to ask if you would speak favorably of me at the court as an applicant for the position? Such a favor would kindle in me only the highest gratitude.

"What do you think?" he asked Vincenzio, "Is this a proper letter?"

Vincenzio read it through. "I couldn't do better myself. Would you like me to mail it for you?"

"No, thank you. I'm going down to meet my friend Rica Baroni, anyway."

Baroni was now a slightly built youth, shorter than Galileo, but dressed more handsomely. His family was wealthy. But Baroni was dissatisfied with the future his father had planned for him.

"Who wants to go into politics?" he asked Galileo, as they walked down the street together. "I want adventure!"

"All I want is to be a professor of mathematics," sighed Galileo. "But I have already been refused by the universities at Bologna and Padua. The letter I just sent off was about the vacancy at Pisa. Perhaps del Monte can help me there."

"That's just what I mean!" cried Rica. "These Italians are an unimaginative lot. Here they have one of the greatest mathematical geniuses since Archimedes under their noses. Do they grab him? No! They let him starve!"

"Now don't exaggerate—"

"Enough! You are always gabbling about the truth! Now, that's the truth, and you know it!" Baroni lowered his voice. "I have some interesting news. Last night, I met a trader from Venice. He had stories to tell that will interest you."

"A trader? What would a trader say to interest me?"

"This man has followed in the footsteps of Marco Polo! He says that the ruler of one of the kingdoms in Persia—the great Shah Abbas—is a powerful patron of the arts and sciences. He has filled Isfahan, his capital city, with great buildings. There is a great university there!"

"What would Persians want with a mathematician?"

"He says that in their university, there are untold opportunities for all learned men!"

"It's something to think about."

"Think of the adventure, man! The mysterious East! Different peoples! Different ways of living! That's the life!"

"Let's wait until I hear about Pisa."

"Pisa, Pisa! Who wants to be in that dull place, when the empires of the East await us?"

Galileo smiled. Rica was so easily bored; he always sought new and exciting things to do. "We'll see, Rica, we'll see."

Baroni poked him. "Don't forget, you're not getting any younger. What is it, twenty-three now?"

"I'll be twenty-five in February."

"There you are! Soon we'll be too old to bend our knees without their cracking! Let's plan for the East now."

"We'll see!"

A month later, Galileo sought out his friend. "Look at this, Rica!"

"What's that, a letter? From Pisa, eh? Looks as though your rich marquis wasn't much help."

"They turned me down! I heard that they gave the post to some older stupid Aristotle worshiper! Well, I'm fed up! What about the East?"

"You mean it? You really want to go?"

"I'm your man!"

Baroni clapped his hands and danced a jig. "I've been thinking about it for weeks. We'll send inquiries by courier post to the court at Isfahan about positions. Meanwhile, I'll contact my trader friend. He can arrange for a vessel to carry us from Venice across the Adriatic Sea. From there, it's onward by camel caravan across the desert to wherever we want to go!"

"One thing, Rica. We must keep this venture a secret until the moment for departure actually arrives."

"Count on me! Think of it, man! Can't you hear the camel bells tinkling away? And those funny humps bobbing up and down? I wonder if you get seasick riding on those beasts!"

Galileo confessed that he had begun to look forward to making his fortune in the mysterious East. "I shall get hold of an Arabic grammar, and we'll study it together."

"A capital idea!"

"Only one thing bothers me—what about money?"

"Have no fear. I have enough for us both."

"But, Rica, I can't let you—"

"I know how things are with you at home, Galileo. Financing this trip is my responsibility, and I want to hear no more about it!"

"But it's not fair—"

"That's enough, I said!"

Galileo threw up his hands. What a wonderful friend Rica was!

* * *

The months of preparation flew by. It was already June. Their departure from Florence was planned for the first day of July. One night, the two conspirators met for a lesson in Arabic. After a few moments of vocabulary practice, Galileo put the book down.

"Rica, I have a confession to make."

"Confess away!"

"The professorship of mathematics at Pisa is vacant again. I have applied for it."

"Is it a sure thing now?"

"Who can tell? I have asked del Monte again to intervene in my behalf."

"He hasn't done much for you up till now."

"I'm sorry, Rica, I had to do it."

"Well, I understand, my friend. But don't get your hopes too high."

"I won't. We'll go on with the plans."

The last day of June came—hot, humid, with a promise of thundershowers. Galileo spent the morning putting aside those possessions he would take to Venice the following day. At noon, he was almost too excited to eat lunch.

"What's the matter with you today?" Madam Giulia was quick to see something was wrong.

"Nothing, Mother."

"Don't try to fool me. You're as jumpy as a hen about to lay an egg."

Galileo could no longer keep the truth from his mother. He told her all about the plans he and Rica had made. On the morrow, they would be off to Venice, and from there— what lay beyond, they did not know.

Madam Giulia shook her head. "Where young people get their ideas nowadays, I don't know. When I was a girl, things were more settled. A boy knew he was going to follow in his father's footsteps, or apprentice himself to a steady, paying profession. Now, all this voyaging about—to the East, to the New World. It's a wonder there are any young people left at home!"

But she had heard that in the East there were fortunes to be made. She told Galileo that he had her blessings for this journey. "But," she added, "it will break your father's heart."

"I think he will understand. After all, I've tried over and over to establish myself in Tuscany. I don't seem to be wanted here at all!"

At that moment, there was the sound of running feet, and Michelangelo burst into the room. "Galileo! Galileo! A letter for you! From Pisa! From the university!"

With trembling hands, Galileo broke open the wax seal stamped with the insignia of the University of Pisa. The letters swam before his eyes, but one sentence he managed to see:

> *. . . to inform you of your appointment to the professorship*
> *of mathematics for the three academic years, 1589 to 1592,*
> *at a yearly salary of sixty florins. Signed by my own hand.*

Drawn with a flourish at the bottom of the page was the signature of the university chancellor.

Galileo just stood there, shaking, until his mother pushed him into a chair.

"I declare, he has fallen into a fit of madness! What kind of news would cause a boy to shiver like that?" Madam Giulia took the letter out of Galileo's hand and squinted at it.

"Such a fine handwriting! So, they are willing to make you a professor at last! But look at the pay! Those thieving scoundrels! Sixty florins! A beggar makes more than that a year scrounging in the public squares!"

"But it's the honor, Mother, more than the money! And it's only a beginning. You'll see. Soon I'll be earning a thousand florins a year and more!"

Madam Giulia handed the letter back to Galileo with a wry expression. "I'll wager there's more to be had in the Kingdom of Persia than in the University of Pisa."

"There's no question about it! I must accept the offer of the university!"

"What about your friend?"

Galileo leaped up. "I had already forgotten about Rica! I must go to him at once and tell him the news." His face fell. "What a mess I will make of his plans!"

But when Baroni heard of Galileo's decision, he was not angry. "What is this nonsense about being sorry? Of course you must take that professorship! It's just what you were intended to be. Now, take me, I'm a made-to-order adventurer. And off to the East I must go!"

"You're going alone?"

"Yes, unless I can find a ready-made partner between now and sunrise."

Galileo's eyes misted with tears, and he wrung Baroni's hand. "Rica—I—you're a true friend. I shall pray every night for your safety and good fortune."

"And I for yours, Galileo." Bidding each other a final adieu, the two friends parted.

That night, there was feasting and joy in the Galilei house. Vincenzio could hardly speak when he first heard the news, he was so overcome. He sent Michelangelo to market for a goose and a large ham. Even Madam Giulia decided the occasion was special enough to bake a large cake with fancy icing on top. With tongue in cheek, she decided upon the decoration on the icing—round candies laid out thus:

The magic triangle of Pythagoras! She had seen Galileo place his pebbles on the floor this way so many times, she knew the shape by heart. The cake was a huge success.

Vincenzio toasted his son. "To the success of the great mathematician of Pisa, Galileo Galilei!" Now he will be bragging about this at the court tomorrow, thought Galileo. But he knew his father's happiness was genuine.

He lifted his glass. "I propose to follow in the footsteps of the great musician Vincenzio Galilei, and to keep the name of Galilei alive in the annals of fame!"

"Oh, what idiots! You are both drunk already! A fine example for the children, Vincenzio!" But Madam Giulia's cheeks were aflame, too, from the glass of red wine she had drunk. After all, a son teaching at the university! One could boast about that to the neighbors.

The delicious goose had been gnawed to the last luscious morsel, and only a small part of the ham clung to the center bone. Madam Giulia and Virginia prepared to clean the table and wash up. Galileo had been thoroughly kissed and hugged and thwacked on the back by everyone. Soon, it was time for bed.

Vincenzio and Galileo stood at the bedroom door. "Son, let me remind you about one thing. I remember how things were at the university when you were a student. Being a faculty member may be more difficult. You can insure good will among them by subscribing to all their ideas. I mean, about Aristotle, and all that."

"What are you saying, Father!"

"Ah, I recognize that tone—it is the voice of the Wrangler! Good, good, that is what I'd hoped you'd say. Stick to the truth, and the devil take their worship of authority! Well, I have no fears about you, so I'll say good night."

"Just one moment, Father." Galileo went back into the living room and got the viola da gamba. "How about 'The White Swan'? Just one chorus, quietly, for me?"

"Well, my voice isn't what it used to be—"

"Please?"

"Very well."

Galileo seated himself with the viola between his legs, placed his fingers in the correct position, and drew the bow gently over the strings.

> *The soft white swan dies singing,*
> *And, weeping, I come to the end of my life.*

As always, Galileo's eyes filled with tears as he listened to the sadness of the words. Looking at Vincenzio, now grown white and a little stooped over with age, Galileo thought he understood the meaning of the song at last.

Suddenly, he was glad that his destination was the University of Pisa, and not the faraway city of Isfahan. Persia was so far from home and all the people he loved.

Chapter V

Galileo was soon caught up in the swirl of university life at Pisa. There were lectures to deliver, faculty meetings to attend, examinations to correct, and conferences with students to be held. There were the academic processions, in which he now marched proudly, wearing the velvet-trimmed robe which marked him as a professor. In whatever spare time he had, he tutored private students for a fee and worked out new mathematical ideas.

Living at the university was like living in a little separate world, cut off from the ordinary affairs of mankind. Here, time went by swiftly, more swiftly than he imagined. He was shocked to realize that almost a year had passed when he received a letter from home telling him of the impending marriage of Virginia to the son of the Tuscan ambassador to Rome. Vincenzio and Madam Giulia were overjoyed; it was an excellent match. One problem, however, remained unsolved. How was Virginia's dowry to be paid? When a girl married, her family was expected to make a substantial gift to her husband. The Galilei family had no way of raising the necessary money.

Galileo realized how embarrassing the whole affair might be for his father. "Have no fear," he wrote to Vincenzio, "I will pledge myself to pay for Virginia's dowry. Meanwhile, I am preparing a surprise wedding present for her. I am having a set of silken bed curtains made for her new home. Say nothing of this to her. I will bring the present myself when I come to Florence for the holidays."

At the university, Galileo was treated rather coldly by most of the professors. They remembered him as the student who had made their lives miserable by asking question after question for which they had no answer. They could not bear to accept him as a colleague. For them, Galileo would always be the Wrangler.

A young philosophy professor, also newly arrived, became his friend. His name was Jacopo Mazzoni. Unlike the others, he listened seriously to what Galileo had to say. And he realized that Galileo's understanding of mathematics and astronomy went far beyond what the average science professor knew.

One day, Galileo asked Mazzoni to visit. "Come to my room. I have something that I think will interest you."

Galileo had been assigned to a little room in a corner of the top floor of the professors' residence building. Up the narrow, dark stairway they went, Galileo leading the way, springing up the steep steps like a mountain goat.

"Whew!" Mazzoni took off his cap and mopped his brow. "Have mercy! This is like climbing the Alps!"

There was little elaborate furniture in Galileo's room—a bed, a table, a chair. But everywhere, on the table, on the chair, and even on the bed, were piles of books. Galileo removed the books from the chair and motioned Mazzoni to sit.

"Jacopo, the key to the mystery is in the pendulum!"

"And what is that remark supposed to mean?" Mazzoni smiled and waited. He was already familiar with the mysterious way in which Galileo loved to announce his new discoveries.

"I have been thinking for many years now about Aristotle's description of the way a body falls down to the ground. Now, what does he say about the speed of falling of such a body, Jacopo?"

"I didn't know this was to be an examination—I would have studied harder, teacher!"

"I'm not fooling!"

"Well, then, everyone knows that the speed is directly related to the weight of the body."

Galileo smiled scornfully. "You mean, everyone believes that a ten-pound weight should fall to the ground ten times faster than a one-pound weight, if they are both released from the same height at the same moment."

Mazzoni nodded.

"Ah, but that is not so!" continued Galileo. "One important thing is wrong. None of these Aristotelians here at Pisa has ever dropped such weights to see if this is true."

Jacopo laughed and slapped his thigh. "It seems to me I heard a story about you and this experiment at a disputation when you were a freshman—"

Galileo grinned. "Oh, I was as green as grass then. I had a hunch something was wrong, but I was too young, too inexperienced." He pointed a finger at Mazzoni. "But now I've got it and I'm sure!"

"Will you please stop talking like a dealer in black magic and come to the point?"

"Very well." Galileo made a swinging motion with his arm. "Doesn't a pendulum represent the motion of a freely falling body?"

Mazzoni pondered a moment. Then his eyes lightened. "Yes, I see what you mean. A ball swinging at the end of a string moves only because of gravity. If there were no string, the ball would fall straight down. But the string keeps it moving from side to side!"

"What a pleasure to talk to you, Jacopo!" Galileo smiled. "Now, then, two pendulums of equal length, but of different weight, should behave as Aristotle said. If one pendulum is ten times the weight of the other, then the heavier pendulum should reach the bottom of its swing ten times faster than the lighter? Am I correct?"

Mazzoni leaned forward with increased interest. "Continue."

"Enough of talking! Let's do the experiment."

Galileo walked to a corner of the room and picked up two balls, one of wood and one of metal. A long string was attached to each. He handed them to Mazzoni. "Feel the difference in weight."

Jacopo balanced one in each hand. "The lead one is certainly ten times heavier than the wooden one."

"Good." Galileo took the makeshift pendulums. "Now I'll attach each of these pendulums to that wooden stud sticking out of the wall up here. Excuse me, Jacopo, I'll need the chair."

Rising, Jacopo hastened to help Galileo fasten the pendulums about a foot apart on the wooden knob. Both strings were exactly the same length. Jumping from the chair,

Galileo pulled the pendulum bobs up, side by side, to the same height.

"Now, Jacopo, when I let go, they will both fall toward the ground at the same time. If Aristotle is correct, the heavier should get to the bottom of the swing before the lighter. Ready?"

Mazzoni nodded eagerly. The pendulum bobs swung down and then moved back and forth freely, but gradually slowing up. From the moment of their release, the bobs remained side by side during all the swings!

"Well, I'll be——!" murmured Mazzoni, his eyes wide with wonder. "Do it again!"

Galileo repeated the experiment. Again both pendulums flashed down and returned upwards together, keeping step as long as they moved.

Mazzoni shook his head. "It's impossible! It's unnatural!"

"No," said Galileo, "what you just saw is *natural!* Aristotle's idea about freely falling bodies is unnatural. What happens, *happens,* Jacopo, no matter what Aristotle says! I have thought about this many nights. I believe that all freely falling bodies fall toward the earth the same way, no matter what their weight."

Mazzoni walked over to the pendulums and toyed with one, letting it swing and bounce against his hand. "But, Galileo, I don't understand——"

"The only thing to understand, Jacopo, is that Pythagoras had the right idea. The working of nature can best be explained by mathematics! Science has been following Aristotle blindly for too many years!"

"You mean that scientists should apply mathematics to the motion of bodies?"

Galileo's eyes gleamed with the light of discovery. "Exactly! If astronomers use mathematics to predict the motions of planets, why can't the laws which govern the movement of bodies on earth be discovered by mathematical measurements? Look here, Jacopo, in mathematics the important thing is to set up the rules of the game first. Then you play according to the rules."

Mazzoni nodded his head to show that he understood.

"Now, what are the important measurements that will allow me to make predictions about motion? I have already discovered them: first, *distance*—how far a body moves; second, *time*—how long it takes a body to move a certain distance; third, *speed*—the change of distance with time; and fourth, *acceleration*—the change of speed with time. On these four quantities, I base my new science of motion!"

"But," asked Mazzoni, "what can your new science accomplish that is different from the old science of Aristotle? Can one do better than to show that the whole universe and man are in harmony with God?"

Eyes gleaming with excitement, Galileo told his friend how the mathematical laws of motion could accomplish deeds that would stagger the imagination. He had already discovered one use for the new science of motion. He could predict the path of a cannon ball from the gun to the target. All that had to be known was the angle at which the gun was aimed!

Mazzoni looked doubtful. "I have a friend who is a cannoneer. He has often told me how difficult it is to fire a cannon ball right on target. It's all a matter of having a practiced eye."

"No more hit-or-miss with my system." Galileo found a piece of paper and a drawing crayon. Falling on his knees, he used the chair seat as a table, talking rapidly as he sketched. "Look here, it's all very simple. There are really two kinds of motion involved in shooting a cannon ball. First, the ball tends to fly out in a straight line. This is the motion given to it by the force of the gunpowder." Galileo drew a straight arrow on the paper.

GUNPOWDER MOTION

"At the same time, gravity tends to pull the cannon ball down toward the ground." Now he joined a downward arrow to the straight one.

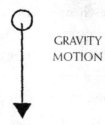

GRAVITY
MOTION

"The actual path of the cannon ball is the result of both of these motions occurring at the same time. This path is a geometrical curve called the parabola." Hastily, Galileo sketched the curve in between the arrows.

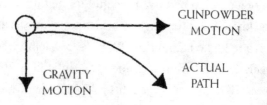

GUNPOWDER
MOTION

ACTUAL
PATH

GRAVITY
MOTION

"If I know the angle at which the gun is aimed, then the mathematics of the parabola allows me to predict quite accurately where the cannon ball will land. If I know the distance from the gun to the target, I can tell the gunner exactly how to aim his gun!"

Mazzoni gazed at the scrap of paper with the diagrams. He scratched his head in wonder. "But if this is true, you will revolutionize military tactics!"

"Oh, that's only one of the results of my new science. I have an entire book about it in my head. As soon as I have time, I shall write it. And this pendulum is the pretty toy that has given me the answers."

Jacopo, however, was levelheaded enough to think of objections. if mathematics was a game played according to rules made by men, he argued, how did Galileo know that this mathematical game would always predict the truth about nature?

"A good question! The answer is, I don't. Then, you may ask, what good is it? Well, the truth about nature and the laws governing its behavior can only be discovered by going directly to nature. Mathematics may point the way, but scientists must begin to do something that has been shunned too long. They must experiment!"

Before Mazzoni could interrupt, Galileo went on. "You see, Aristotle's laws of nature are not based on experiments. We still believe that wise men should use their tongues, not their hands! But the only way I can find out if my mathematical laws are true is to see if they predict what really happens. I must make pendulums, drop weights, measure time and distance. Any science about nature must begin and end with experience itself!"

"But," Mazzoni protested, "this is against all—"

"Against all recognized authority?" interrupted Galileo. "You are right. But the followers of Aristotle have always been concerned with *why* things happen. If you ask only *why*, as a child usually does, what kind of an answer can you expect? I call them *because* answers. 'Because it's so!' Such an answer leads nowhere. But if you ask *how* something happens, there is a strange and wonderful difference. *How* questions lead to mathematical answers, to predictions, to new *how* questions, to new mathematical answers—there is an endless chain of new knowledge!"

Galileo seemed so sure of himself, Mazzoni found himself almost believing that the mathematical picture of nature was true. Yet, the university training he had received in Aristotelian science was so ingrained that he had to ask again how Galileo knew.

"I just know this is the truth, Jacopo! The mathematical picture of how freely falling bodies fall to earth agrees so beautifully with Pythagorean number magic that I know this must be the way God meant nature to act! You remember the magic number triangles?"

Mazzoni nodded. How could he forget? They were one and three and six and ten.

"Now, then!" Galileo took the piece of paper from Mazzoni's hand and began to put down numbers. "In order to make the triangles, two pebbles are added first, then three pebbles, then four. This is the sequence of our way of counting: one, two, three, four. Strangely enough—or perhaps not so strangely—the speed of a freely falling body increases this way in equal intervals of time. At the end of a second of falling, for example, a stone will have a speed of thirty-two feet per second. At the end of two seconds, the speed is doubled—sixty-four feet per second—and so on!"

Entranced, Mazzoni could only blink his eyes to show he understood.

Galileo continued: "That's the first relationship. For the second, I have to remind you about the Pythagorean squares." Galileo hunted in a corner until he found the bag of white stones. Kneeling, he began to place them on the floor as he talked.

"We begin with one stone."

O

"Now to make a square, I add three stones."

O O
O O

"For the next square, I add five stones."

O O O
O O O
O O O

"Then, I add seven."

O O O O
O O O O
O O O O
O O O O

"I follow the sequence there," said Mazzoni. "You start with one, then come three, five, seven—the odd numbers."

"Yes. In the case of the freely falling body, the speeds follow the sequence of the Pythagorean triangles. But the distances fallen through in equal intervals of time differ in the sequence of the Pythagorean squares! In the first second, a stone will fall sixteen feet; in the second, it will fall three times sixteen, or forty-eight feet; in the third, it will fall five times sixteen—"

Mazzoni shook his head. "This is all so new—so wonderful—I don't know what to say!"

"Don't you think this agreement with Pythagorean numbers is not just an accident?"

Mazzoni admitted that it was as though Pythagorean number magic was part of nature.

Galileo sighed. "If I could only persuade my superiors here as easily as I have convinced you. But those old fools will not—"

Mazzoni placed a warning finger across Galileo's lips. To speak ill of the senior professors was a most disrespectful act, and might cost a younger professor his position. Galileo checked himself and laughed.

"I suppose you are right, Jacopo. But they make me so angry, I could—" He crashed his fist on the table so hard that the books jumped into the air. "What's the use! They are so soaked in Aristotle that they cannot think for themselves. Come on, let's go. It's my turn to buy dinner."

Pulling Mazzoni by the hand, Galileo plunged down the winding staircase. At the bottom, they almost crashed into a stooped, venerable figure wearing the velvet robe of a full professor. The old man, balance recovered, waved his wooden staff angrily.

"Young scamps!" Indignantly, he reset his flat black cap over the few silver hairs on his almost bald pate. "I don't know what universities are coming to. This generation has no respect for—"

He paused, blinking pale blue watery eyes at the two instructors. "Why, it's Mazzoni! And you, Master Galileo! Such dashing about, almost knocking people down, is more the kind of conduct I would expect from first-year students!"

"A thousand pardons, sir," said Galileo sweetly, bowing his head, "but you see, only a moment ago we were discussing motion itself with such ardor that we threw ourselves into active motion down the stairs."

"Careful!" muttered Mazzoni into Galileo's ear. "The head of the philosophy department has little stomach for jokes."

"How interesting that you should mention motion." The old professor gazed out into space as though trying to recall something. Then he flung one arm out and declaimed, "A body which has a greater weight than a second body falls more swiftly through the air than the second, and the speeds of the two bodies are in a ratio to their weight! That's from Aristotle's book, *Physica*, you know. What a delightful disputation we had about it today in the philosophy class!"

"But, sir," asked Galileo, "wouldn't it have been more fruitful to have discussed such a statement in the mathematics class?"

"Mathematics? But you are joking, of course!"

"Not at all." Galileo pulled free from the restraining grip of Mazzoni. "Mathematics can show that this statement is completely wrong."

"What? What? Did I hear you say 'wrong'?" The Aristotelian professor shook his head in disbelief. "You mean to say that Aristotle is wrong?"

"Yes, sir! The mathematics of a freely falling body shows that all bodies must fall to the ground with the same increasing swiftness, regardless of weight."

"What? What? I don't understand! Mazzoni! Here, now, what do you make of this talk?"

Mazzoni gulped and stuttered a few unintelligible words.

"Oh, now, sir, don't ask Jacopo! He doesn't understand it at all yet. But, please, listen for yourself. Hear my arguments, if only for a few moments, sir!"

"Well—" The professor motioned for Galileo to speak. The young mathematician repeated all that he had told Mazzoni upstairs about swinging pendulums and freely falling bodies. The old man listened patiently for a while. Gradually, however, he began to fidget with impatience. Soon, he interrupted, roaring at Galileo in great indignation.

"Pythagorean numbers? Squares? A new science of motion? Why, young man, this is the rankest nonsense I have ever been forced to hear!"

"But other well-known philosophers have questioned Aristotle on this matter!" Galileo was fighting angry now, shouting back at the professor. "What about John Philoponus, who was a great teacher over thirteen hundred years ago? He tried the experiment of dropping two different weights from the same height. And he found that they both struck the ground at the same time. I read that with my own eyes in his book about Aristotle! And then there is the great mathematician Jerome Cardan, dead only these thirteen years.

In his last book, *The New Book of Proportions,* he proves that two balls of the same material, but differing in weight, when dropped from the same height, must strike the ground at the same moment!"

"The devil take your mathematicians!" cried the Aristotelian. "Their books mean nothing to me! I once saw some fool dropping weights in this manner. And the heavier weight arrived at the ground first. Am I not to believe Aristotle when I see this with my own eyes?"

"But the shape of the body makes a difference!" Galileo could feel Mazzoni's anxious fingers plucking at his sleeve, but he paid no attention. "Look here, I'll do the experiment for you right now!"

He fished in his pocket and came up with a florin. "Here we have a metal coin—a heavy body. Let me have that book, Jacopo." Galileo tore one of the blank filler pages from the back of the book, while Mazzoni watched in horror. "And here is a rectangle of paper—a light body. We let them fall from the same height at exactly the same moment."

The coin fell straight to the ground, while the paper twirled slowly downward.

"You see! You see!" shouted the professor. "You confound yourself, young man! The heavier body outruns the lighter by far!"

"One moment." Galileo picked up the coin and paper. "Now let me change the *shape* of the lighter body." He crumpled the paper into a little ball. "The weight is still the same, of course. Now I drop them again."

This time, the coin struck only a fraction of a second ahead of the paper wad.

"But the heavier body still struck the ground first, just as Aristotle predicts!" shouted the professor.

"But hardly in the same way, my dear colleague," retorted Galileo. "The coin was more than ten times heavier than the paper, but it did not reach the ground in one tenth the time. The very small difference you saw was caused by the greater resistance of the air to the paper. If the experiment could be done in a space where there is no air—in a vacuum—the coin and the paper would strike at the same moment both times."

"Ohhhh!" groaned Mazzoni, like a man with a stomach ache. "What a time to talk about a vacuum!"

"A vacuum! Did you hear, Mazzoni? He talks of a vacuum! Doesn't he know his Aristotle? *Natura horror vacui!* Nature abhors a vacuum! There can be no such thing as a space full of nothing! Why, look here! Aristotle tells us that the speed with which a body falls to earth depends upon the *medium* through which it falls. A stone falls faster through air than through water. But if the stone fell in a vacuum, through *nothing*, it would fall with endless speed. In fact, all bodies of all weights would fall with the same endless speed. Now, common sense tells us that such a thing cannot happen! Therefore, a vacuum cannot exist! Bear me out, Mazzoni, is it not written so in Aristotle?"

"Oh, y-yes, sir, you are right, sir, absolutely right!" Mazzoni was torn between aiding Galileo and supporting his superior, but it seemed wiser to be polite to the old man, whose power in the university was great.

"That, sir, is mathematical nonsense!" cried Galileo.

"Now I must be called a speaker of nonsense! The younger generation has no respect, no respect! The Rector shall hear of this insult, sir! Good day, Mazzoni!"

Muttering to himself, the old professor stomped away, striking his walking staff upon the ground with sharp cracks.

Mazzoni wiped the perspiration from his brow. "I'd better go after him, Galileo. His anger will do us no good." He turned to follow the chief professor.

"Go, go! I should have known better than to waste time on a stubborn old fool!" Galileo turned angrily and strode up the street.

"Galileo! Ho, there! Galileo!"

He looked for the voice. It came from a figure far down the street, near the main gate of the university. The figure waved its hands as it came nearer. Galileo could see it was a man.

"Galileo! It is I, Ostilio Ricci!"

"Ostilio!" Galileo embraced the older mathematician. "Man, it is good to see you! Wait until you hear the results of my new work with the pendulum! I have—"

"That can wait. I am afraid I am the bearer of bad news, my friend. Your father is dead!"

Tears sprang into Galileo's eyes. "Dead? But—but only last week I had a letter from him . . . he wrote he was well . . . I don't understand—"

"It happened two days ago. A sudden stroke, and he was gone. Just like that! I am sorry. He was a fine and intelligent man. And above all, he was a good friend."

Galileo could not speak. He stood there, as if in a trance, until Ostilio gently led him back to his room.

That night, Galileo sat up late, writing a letter to Madam Giulia:

. . . I wish I could come, but I must lecture tomorrow. As you know, if I am absent for any reason, the time is deducted from my salary. There is little enough left as it is. But I am sending you a few florins to help pay funeral expenses. Have no fears for the future, dear Mother. Some time ago, I promised Father that if anything happened to him, I would take care of you. I will arrange for some kind of monthly allowance for you and the children. As for Virginia's dowry, that will have to wait awhile. Keep your courage up. Mother, I will not forget my promise . . .

His pen stopped. Galileo sat staring at the candle flame for a long time. Now he was a man with heavy responsibilities. His carefree days were over.

Chapter VI

The days began to pass more quickly. Galileo spent more of his time designing and performing new experiments with moving bodies. But something began to go wrong at the university. Fewer students came to his classes. In the lecture hall, hisses began to be heard when he attacked the scientific ideas of Aristotle. He felt as though the whole university had turned against him.

"It's no use, Jacopo!" Galileo and Mazzoni were walking along the broad avenue that led to the university. "No one really wants me here! I'm going to resign!"

"What kind of foolish talk is this? Resign? Why, you're the best mathematics lecturer they've had in years! Besides, it's still half a year before our contracts expire."

"I don't care about the contract! I'm shaking the dust of Pisa from my heels! I wish I had gone to Isfahan with my friend Baroni! Who would have thought that such a great university would be governed by such small minds? This is no place for someone who is searching for truth!"

"But where will you go? What will you do?"

"Back to Florence, I guess. I'll find something—pupils, a private school. After all, I have something of a reputation. Perhaps I'll petition the Grand Duke—"

"I wish you would reconsider—" Mazzoni stopped and looked deep into Galileo's eyes. "No, I see you are quite

determined, and nothing I can say will stop you. Well—"
He seized Galileo's hand and gripped it firmly. "I shall be
sorry to see you go. You are the one good friend I have here.
And with you will go all those pleasant hours of stimulating
talk—oh, how I shall miss that!"

"So will I, Jacopo, so will I!"

Galileo placed his hand on Mazzoni's shoulder in a gesture of farewell. Sadly, the two friends parted.

When Galileo returned to the little house in Florence,
Madam Giulia expressed her opinions quite bluntly.

"Oh, if only I hadn't listened to your father! By now you
would be on your way to riches. Why didn't we apprentice
you to Marco Pontelli!"

"Don't worry, Mother. I have some pupils to tutor. And I
shall soon find another position."

"But look how long it took you to get this one at Pisa! And
now you've given it up, just like that! Galileo Galilei, I don't
understand you, I just don't!"

The problem of money was becoming a vexing one.
Michelangelo had become a fine musician, thanks to
Vincenzio's teaching. He had many friends, sons of noblemen and rich merchants. But he hated work, and spent his
time playing and singing instead of acquiring paying pupils.
He was very vain, and insisted that Galileo buy him elegant
clothing so that he would not shame his friends.

Livia was already outgrowing her clothes and insisting
that Virginia's hand-me-downs were out of fashion. And the
price of food was so high! Madam Giulia complained that
she could not make both ends meet on the money Galileo
brought in.

One morning in September, Galileo fought bitterly with Michelangelo over an expensive ermine-trimmed hat the latter had bought with the money he should have spent for a new lute. Galileo flung the hat to the floor, and Michelangelo stamped out of the house in a rage. At noon, Livia came home in tears, because her friends had made fun of her clothes. She insisted that Galileo had to buy her a new dress and new shoes at once.

"See how your brother and sister are ashamed before their own friends!" Madame Giulia spoke harshly. "What will become of us?"

Galileo knew that his mother could not help her scolding ways—it was just her nature. He realized that she really loved him very much and worried about him. But on this day, her accusations were just too much for him. He was about to reply angrily, when there was a knock on the door. It was a special messenger from the Marquis del Monte with a letter. Swallowing the bitter words he had been on the point of uttering, Galileo tore the letter open.

> *Greetings, dear friend:*
>
> *I write in haste to tell you that the chair of mathematics at the University of Padua in the Republic of Venice is still vacant. I have approached the authorities with the suggestion that you are the one to fill the post properly. I believe that if you hasten to Venice at once for a personal interview with the authorities, the position will be yours. Stop at Padua on the way and see my good friend Gianvincenzo Pinelli. He is a man of great influence in Venetian affairs and can help you. Do not delay. Professor Magini of the University of Bologna*

has also applied for the position. He, too, has many friends. But this time, I think you have more. Good fortune and best wishes.

Within an hour, Galileo had borrowed a horse, kissed his family good-by, and was galloping to the northeast, toward Padua.

The journey took two days, though he pushed his horse to the limits of its endurance. He spent the night at a wretched little inn where a sparse supper of bread and cheese and a sack of straw for a bed cost him half a florin, paid in advance. He lay awake most of the night, tossing with anxiety and discomfort. With the first rays of the sun, he was up. Before anyone else at the inn was awake, he had splashed cold well water on his face and was on his way.

Late that afternoon, the roofs of Padua appeared on the horizon. The city was larger than Pisa, but did not appear too different. The University of Padua, Galileo knew, was larger than the one at Pisa and more famous for its scholars.

It did not take him long to find Pinelli, a fat little man who lived in a white marble palace. Pinelli greeted Galileo with a welcoming smile and a hearty handshake. He ordered food to be brought. While Galileo ate like a starving man, Pinelli outlined their program for the following day.

"I'll take del Monte's word," he said. "If he says you are the man for the job, then that's it. You will stay the night here. Tomorrow, we depart for Venice in my carriage. Leave your horse in my stables—I imagine the poor beast is worn out. Now tell me about your problems at Pisa."

While Galileo described the actions of his enemies at the university, Pinelli shook his head and nodded and clucked in sympathy.

"Have no fears about Padua, Galileo. You will find that things are different in the Republic of Venice."

Venice! Galileo had heard about this fabulous city where the main streets were all canals, but he was not prepared for the beauty that burst upon him the following day.

Rows of ornate houses and palaces rose from the very waters themselves. The colors were magnificent. There were white marble and stones painted red, blue, and yellow. The roofs were of bright red tile. Gilt figures hung on the walls, and all about was the blue of the water. Exquisite stone bridges crisscrossed the canals at intervals.

The water was alive with boat traffic. Pinelli named the different kinds of boats for him: gondolas, with their ends curving up like Turkish crescents; *piottas*, small flat-bottomed boats moved by oarsmen; and the *barchiellos*, great barges with canvas roofs, that ferried as many as twenty people at a time to different parts of the city.

Their carriage stopped at a small pier. Pinelli motioned Galileo toward a gondola, and they both stepped aboard. The gondolier was a swarthy man with a large mustache and very white teeth. Perched on his head was a red stocking cap with a long tassel. Galileo noticed that he wore no shoes. Pinelli gave the order: "To Saint Mark's Square."

The gondolier saluted and swung his long oar. They moved smoothly through the water. The gondolier hummed to himself as he plied his oar back and forth, skillfully avoiding collisions with the many other boats moving up and down the canal. Occasionally, Galileo heard a loud splash. Once he looked up and spied a housewife emptying her garbage bucket right into the canal waters.

When he mentioned this to Pinelli, the latter shrugged. "What harm does it do? The water is salt and cleans all foul odors away. Our drinking water comes from wells outside the city—there can be no pollution."

As they neared the landing at Saint Mark's Square, Galileo could see out into the harbor. It was filled with small fishing vessels with multicolored sails. They skimmed among many high-masted ships, some coming, some outward bound, some waiting at wharves to be loaded or unloaded. Their great sails sparkled white in the sun. Galileo thought of his friend Rica Baroni, and the time when they had planned to sail from this very harbor on one of those ships to the faraway lands of the East. I wonder if Rica has found the adventure he pursued, he thought.

Saint Mark's Square was a great open space, paved with long rows of colored bricks set in herringbone pattern. The marble columns and arches of the palace of the Doge, the elected leader of the republic, faced the harbor. Beside it sparkled the white domes and spires of Saint Mark's Church. Over all towered the campanile, the bell tower, commanding a view of the entire city.

Galileo and Pinelli stepped out of the gondola into a hubble-bubble of human activity. People were parading back and forth across the square, conversing in pairs and groups. Galileo saw one strange thing that made him laugh out loud. When Pinelli turned to him questioningly, Galileo pointed.

"Those shoes! I have never seen anything like them!"

He was staring at the shoes of a noblewoman who had just passed. The soles of her shoes were wooden platforms over a foot high! The woman tottered, rather than walked, leaning on the arm of a companion. As he looked about him, Galileo saw that all the women in the square wore similar shoes, some slightly lower, but some even higher!

Pinelli smiled. "An old Venetian custom. Many years ago, the little streets here were unpaved and muddy. So, the women of Venice began to wear shoes that would lift them out of the mud. Well, you know how women are. Suddenly it became the fashion to walk on shoes that were like stilts. Actually, there is a law which forbids such an extravagance, but no one pays attention to it."

"The women of Venice ought to read my essay on the center of gravity of bodies. It would help them to keep their balance."

Galileo's eyes kept wandering from one side of the square to the other. There were so many new things to be seen! He noticed that men and women were more handsomely dressed here than in Pisa.

A religious procession moved slowly out of the center door of Saint Mark's and began to circle the square. First came the choristers, holding their hymnals and singing. Then followed some church dignitaries, dressed in long white robes and walking with a solemn air. Some of them carried small statues of saints. Behind them marched a double row of gray-clad monks. Each monk held a tall white candle, lighted and set in a silver candlestick.

The mathematician and the businessman paused a moment to pay their respects to the procession. Then Pinelli tugged at Galileo's sleeve. "This way. We'd better hurry. They're expecting us."

Pinelli halted before the iron door of a stone palace whose balconied windows rose three stories above the water. He raised the heavy knocker shaped like a lion's head and let it fall. After a moment, the door opened, and a tall man dressed in a monk's robe stood there. Above the simple brown robe Galileo saw a handsome face, with a strong hooked nose and dark deep-set eyes. He wore a carefully clipped mustache and a short pointed beard in the latest fashion. Galileo's impression was that here was a man of unusual intelligence and strong convictions.

"Ah, Sarpi, it's you," said Pinelli. "Are you acting as doorman today?" He shook the monk's hand and introduced Galileo.

"Here is our mathematician. Galileo, this is Brother Paolo Sarpi. And don't let that simple monk's robe fool you. He knows as much as most of the university professors put together."

Sarpi laughed, showing fine white teeth. "Come in and welcome, Signor Galileo. I have read your treatise on the center of gravity. It is an excellent work that tells me you have promise of a great future. And of course we all know about your pulse-beat measurer. But pay little attention to Pinelli. He tends to chatter like a magpie!"

Galileo could see from the way the two men joked with each other that they were fast friends. Brother Sarpi led the way into a lavishly furnished sitting room. There were two other men in the room. One was elderly, with a bald head and white beard; the other was about Galileo's age, perhaps a few years younger.

"Signer Galileo, this is Professor Gerolamo Fabrizio of the Medical School at the University of Padua. You may have heard his name spoken at Pisa."

Galileo was overwhelmed. "Who has not heard of the great Fabricius of Acquapendente?" He used the physician's Latinized name. University professors often signed the books and papers they wrote with a Latin version of their names, together with the town of birth. Galileo shook Fabrizio's hand warmly. "Perhaps, if you had been my anatomy teacher at Pisa, I might have remained a medical student."

The eyes of the famous anatomist were clear and searching. But now their corners crinkled in a smile. "Then I am glad I was teaching at Padua! For had you become a physician, the Pulsilogia might never have been given to medicine. You can't imagine what a boon your invention has been to the diagnosis of disease. I hope we can become friends."

To receive such a compliment from so great a man made Galileo blush. *How I wish Vincenzio were in this room to hear this,* he thought; *how proud he would be!*

"And this is Gianfresco Sagredo." Sarpi was introducing the younger man.

"Oh, how I have looked forward to this day!" exclaimed Sagredo. Without pausing for breath, he began to ply Galileo with questions about Copernican astronomy.

"Gianfresco! Give the man a chance to catch his breath!" cried Pinelli.

"No matter. I don't mind answering his questions." Galileo, feeling somewhat flattered, tried to put the blushing youth at ease.

"This is the palace of Sagredo's parents," explained Sarpi. "He is a young man with an extremely inquisitive mind. Wait until he shows you his animal room—dozens of strange creatures—and they're all alive!"

"I'd like very much to see that room." Galileo began to relax in the company of these friendly, learned people.

"You will have time for this kind of tomfoolery later," Pinelli interrupted. "Now we must prepare you to go before the Riformatori."

"Who are they?" asked Galileo.

"In Venice," explained Brother Sarpi, "the control of the university and the whole system of national schools and libraries is given over to three learned noblemen. They are elected for two-year terms, and all teacher candidates must be examined by them."

"Good Lord!" exclaimed Galileo. "I haven't prepared anything special to talk about—"

"Have no fears," soothed Pinelli. "They may appear to be very pedantic and dignified men, but they are really very kind. And I happen to know that in the realm of mathematics their learning is not so great. They may ask you some questions about grammar, about Aristotle's nonscientific philosophy, or about Latin authors—"

Galileo sighed with relief. "I'm not afraid of those questions."

"We'll all come with you and lend moral support," put in Sagredo. Brother Sarpi led the way to the door, where they were bowed out by a liveried footman. In a few moments, they had all boarded Pinelli's gondola and were threading their way through the canal traffic.

The three Riformatori stood in the center of what Galileo thought was the largest and most beautiful room he had ever seen. The walls were hung with great colorful tapestries depicting scenes in the history of Venice, and the furniture was decorated with gold. The Riformatori wore long robes of purple velvet. Two of them had black stoles over their shoulders. The third, an older man with a long white beard, wore an exquisite cape of gold cloth.

Pinelli advanced and bowed. "Gentlemen, I wish to present to you the well-known mathematician of Florence, Signor Galileo Galilei."

Galileo felt a few butterflies in his stomach for a moment. Then he decided that if he had not been afraid of the professors at the University of Pisa, there was no reason to fear these three Venetians.

"Come forward, please, Signor Galilei," said the eldest of the Riformatori. "Now, tell me," he added, when Galileo had moved out into the center of the room, "what do you think of Cicero's essay on old age?"

Galileo, who had read this essay many times over with Father Paul at Vallombrosa, was able to give a very learned opinion. The old man nodded approvingly and signed to one of his colleagues to ask the next question. The questioning continued for an hour. Finally, the eldest Riformatori said hesitantly, "Now, as for mathematics and astronomy—"

Sarpi stepped forward quickly. "If it please you, sir, Signor Pinelli and myself can vouch for Signor Galilei's unusual ability and excellence in those areas of knowledge. As you may know, he comes well recommended by the Marquis del Monte, who is a mathematician of no small means himself."

"Hrrmmph! Of course! Well—" The Riformatori waved his hand in dismissal. "You may be seated over there while we discuss this matter."

It did not take the three long to reach a decision. One of them went to a side door and rang a little bell that hung there. As he did this, the elder turned and motioned for Galileo to come forward again.

The old man drew himself up to his full height. Galileo could see that he was very much concerned with the solemnity and importance of the occasion.

"Hrrmmph! It is my pleasure, young man, to inform you that the decision of the Riformatori of the Republic of Venice is that you—hrrmmph!—shall be appointed professor of mathematics and astronomy in the University of Padua. Hrrmmph!"

Galileo's friends came forward to congratulate him. They all shook his hand vigorously, and Sagredo clapped him joyously on the back. "Hurrah for science at Padua!"

Just then the door opened, and the clerk came in. He was a thin little man, with a long face and a bulbous nose. Perched on it was a pair of narrow spectacles, through which he peered at a large piece of parchment covered with elegant script.

"Will you please read the contract aloud for Signer Galilei?" asked the eldest Riformatori. Galileo knew now that his being selected for the professorship at Padua had been prearranged.

The clerk tended to bumble through his nose when he spoke. "Now—ha, hum—on this twenty-sixth of September, 1592, there has been found Signor Galileo Galilei, who lectured previously at the University of Pisa with very great honor and success—"

Little enough honor, thought Galileo, remembering the cold glances of the professors at Pisa, and the hisses when he had lectured.

"—and who may be considered the first in his profession. Since he is ready and willing to come to our university— hmm . . . and so on . . . it is proper to accept him. Therefore, the said Galileo Galilei is hereby appointed professor of mathematics in our university for four years—hmmm . . . and so on . . . with the yearly salary of one hundred and eighty florins—" He peered over his spectacles. "That salary is, of course, acceptable?"

Galileo's heart leaped. Acceptable? It was three times as much as he had received at Pisa! He nodded dumbly.

The clerk finished reading. "Ha, hum—signed with our hands this day, in accordance with our authority as Riformatori of the Republic of Venice—hmmm . . . and so on . . . sign here please!"

Hand trembling with excitement, Galileo traced the letters of his name on the parchment. It was the proudest and happiest day of his life.

"This is a great occasion for Padua and Venice," said Brother Sarpi. The Riformatori, nodding their heads solemnly, agreed with him. "How soon can you come to Padua?" asked one of them.

"Why, I hadn't thought about it! I suppose I must return to Florence to get permission to come and live in Padua."

"Ah, yes. Going from one Italian state to another is such a tiring business. So many formalities."

"Have no fear," put in Pinelli. "I'll see that everything goes through without a hitch."

"And there's my family to settle before I leave. It might take a month or so. I'm their only provider, you see——" Galileo hesitated, seemingly embarrassed.

"What is it. Signor Galilei?" asked the elder Riformatori.

"Well, I didn't want to ask—it's about deductions, sir. At Pisa, all absences were deducted from my salary. One time, when my mother was ill, I went home for two weeks—it cost me five and one half florins! So, I didn't know whether——"

"Bah!" roared the Riformatori, anger breaking through his veneer of dignity. "Do you compare us to those Tuscan misers at Pisa? We treat our professors as noble, learned men, not as indentured apprentices! You may have all the time you wish to settle your affairs. Nothing will be deducted from your salary. Oh, those Pisans—what a way to run a university!"

Galileo felt better. Still, he felt he should clear his mind of all doubts. "There's one other thing, sir."

"Well?"

"The things said about me in the contract were very flattering indeed. But I am a great believer in the truth, sir, and I think you should know that my ideas about science were rather unpopular at Pisa. Perhaps some of your faculty may resent—"

Sarpi stepped forward. "I can answer for that, Galileo, You have nothing to fear at Padua. There, truth and knowledge are respected. You will be free to search for the truth in any way you wish!"

Galileo's heart was full. He grasped Sarpi's hand in gratitude. "Thank you, dear friend. Since the death of my father, I thought I would never hear such words spoken again!"

When Galileo left Venice, he was filled with a warm glow of good fellowship and friendliness. This is the place I have dreamed about all my life, he thought, as he jogged homeward toward Florence. At Padua, I will at last find understanding—and truth.

Chapter VII

In the twenty-eighth year of his life, in Padua, a golden time began for Galileo.

With his increased salary, he was able to rent a small house near the university. Here he could work, entertain his friends, and tutor private pupils at his leisure. He soon discovered that Brother Sarpi had been right. At the University of Padua, most of the teachers understood that the search for knowledge could not be separated from the search for truth.

Galileo began to work very hard. He was interested in almost everything—machines, motion, the stars and planets, painting, and even poetry. Paper after paper on different subjects streamed from his pen. He wrote a paper on military buildings and fortifications, though he had never been a soldier. He wrote a paper on the science of machines, in which he glorified the work of Archimedes. He wrote a short paper on the acceleration of falling bodies, and planned to turn this into a great book. Galileo's papers were copied and sent to universities and royal courts all over Europe. In a few years, the name of Galileo was on everyone's lips.

His greatest joy, however, was in his newfound friends. He found that Brother Sarpi was, as Pinelli had said, a very learned scientist. Galileo made it a point to discuss all his new ideas with Sarpi. The businessman, Pinelli, also proved to be a valuable friend.

Galileo had never forgotten the day when Pinelli asked him to visit his palace. After the footman had conducted Galileo to the vast parlor, with its vast furnishings, Pinelli had beckoned him over to a side door.

"I have a surprise for you." He flung open the door and motioned Galileo inside.

Galileo found himself in a great room, unlike any he had ever seen before. The walls, from floor to ceiling, were covered with books, thousands and thousands of books. There were no libraries for public use, where anyone who wanted to read could just go in and borrow a book. Such collections of books were luxuries that only very, very rich people could afford. Otherwise, they were to be found only in universities and monasteries.

"This is my private library," said Pinelli. "I've never had them counted, but I believe there are about eighty thousand books here. You are welcome to use this as your own. Come as often as you wish. Borrow as many as you want."

Being in a library of this size was, for Galileo, something like being in heaven. He spent many happy hours reading in Pinelli's library, always finding something new, storing countless ideas in his mind.

Young Sagredo established himself firmly as Galileo's aide and protector. He was always to be found in Galileo's home, reading, asking questions, drinking in knowledge as fast as he was able. If anyone even dared to hint that Galileo was not the greatest scientist in the world, he had to answer to a fighting Sagredo.

The three companions, Galileo, Sarpi, and Sagredo, spent many happy hours eating, drinking, and singing together. The great physician, Fabrizio, also became a good friend to Galileo, but in a different way. Their friendship began when Galileo became his patient.

It was on a hot day during Galileo's first summer in Padua. The fierce rays of the sun seemed to scorch everything they touched. Even just sitting in the house was very uncomfortable. Two young university instructors, new acquaintances, came by Galileo's house and invited him to accompany them on a picnic into the nearby countryside.

Galileo agreed. "At least, it should be cooler there."

But the countryside, too, was unbearably hot. It became an effort for them to walk along the little road that led away from Padua. Around a bend in the road, they came to the entrance of a large country house, evidently the home of some wealthy person.

"Wait a moment," said one of the instructors, "I know who lives here. This is the villa of the Count da Trento. He is a good friend of my father. Perhaps he will allow us to come in and rest out of the sun." He led the way to the door of the villa.

As the instructor had predicted, the Count made them all welcome. He had refreshing cold drinks brought. When they complained about how hot and tired they had become during their walk, he said, "I have a wonderfully cool place where you can rest. It is a room cooled by cold air that comes from an underground tunnel."

He led them down a stairway into a room that had no windows. But, from behind a curtained section of wall, a cool stream of air issued forth. In the room were comfortable lounges and cots. Bidding them to remain there as long as they wished, the Count left them. Stretching out with sighs and exclamations over the comforts of the lounges, the three fell asleep.

Galileo awoke with a strange feeling of uneasiness and discomfort. His throat burned, and all his joints seemed to ache. He barely managed to stagger to his feet and stumble over to where the two instructors slept. He could not rouse them. Somehow he reached the doorway and shouted hoarsely before he slumped to the floor in a faint.

Many days passed before he regained consciousness. He awoke, aware only of a blur and a firm hand sponging his brow. Then his eyes focused, and the blur became the white beard and the benevolent face of Fabrizio. The worried look went out of the physician's eyes.

"Welcome back to the living, Galileo."

Galileo tried to ask, "What happened?" But only a guttural croak came from his lips.

"Don't try to talk. You have been very sick. But now, the Lord be praised, you will recover."

"—others?" Galileo managed to gasp.

"I'll tell you everything later. All you have to worry about now is getting better. Here, drink a little of this." He lifted a cup to Galileo's lips. Galileo managed to sip a bit of the sweet, brackish medicine before he fell asleep.

Later, he learned that the two young teachers had died from being exposed, while overheated and exhausted, to the damp, cold air of the underground room. He had been lucky. God had spared him. Galileo mourned for his unfortunate colleagues. He could not shake a feeling of guilt for their deaths.

"Nonsense!" said Fabrizio severely. "No one was responsible, except nature herself. You were fortunate to have a stronger resistance to the effects of the sudden chilling of your blood. Anyway," he smiled, "Sarpi threatened to skin me alive if I didn't save you. I had no choice."

"How did I get back to Padua?"

"The Count da Trento heard you call. He had the three of you rushed here by carriage. One of the youths had already gone when you arrived—the other died a few days later. You had a high fever, and I despaired of your life."

"But you never left my side for four days and nights, until the fever began to leave me. I know all about it. Sagredo told me." Galileo took Fabrizio's hand. "And I am grateful for such a wonderful friend."

The physician snorted. He disliked a show of emotion. "Bah, that Sagredo! He talks too much!" He looked at Galileo and spoke more seriously. "I must warn you in all frankness that there may be consequences. You may have occasional aches in your joints. Send for me any time you feel any discomfort." He did not tell Galileo that he would suffer from the effects of his exposure for the rest of his life.

As soon as Galileo was well enough to resume his duties at the university, he plunged back into his work. Many private pupils came to him for tutoring. Padua was a university with an international flavor. Pupils came from all over the world. It was at the University of Padua, only a hundred years before, that the young Copernicus had come from Poland to find those seeds of thought which had later flourished into the theory that the sun was the center of the world.

Custom demanded that Galileo teach, in his astronomy lectures, that system of the world in which the earth stood unmoving in the center of the world, while the sun circled about it. Nevertheless, Galileo believed that the idea of Copernicus was more accurate. But there was really no way to tell which of the two systems was the better one. The mathematics of Copernicus made predicting the movements of some of the planets a bit easier. But his mathematics was much more difficult than the mathematics of the Ptolemaic world. Few astronomers had patience enough to learn the new methods. And common sense indicated that the sun moved, not the earth.

However, Galileo's belief in the Copernican system was so strong that he began to teach both methods in his lectures. He waited for someone to criticize him publicly. He expected to be hissed by the Aristotelians. But, to his surprise, the reverse of what happened at Pisa took place. Students and faculty alike crowded the lecture hall to hear him speak. Soon Galileo was given the honor of lecturing in the largest hall in the university, the lecture room called the Aula Magna.

One morning there was a knock on his door. To Galileo's surprise, it was Michelangelo.

"What are you doing here?"

"That's not much of a greeting for your dear brother."

"It's just that I'm surprised to see you."

"Well, since you ask, I have come to Padua to seek my fortune."

"Come in, come in. You can tell me about it sitting down."

Michelangelo had with him a large traveling trunk full of elaborate clothing, and his lutes. Galileo helped him drag the trunk into the house. "Oof! You have enough stuff in here to clothe a troupe of players!"

"I have discovered that one must have the proper clothes to get along in noble society."

"Yes," muttered Galileo under his breath, "my purse knows all about that." Out loud he said, "Do you have any plans?"

"I have heard that there are many rich foreigners who come to the university as students. I thought you might be able to help me find some music pupils among them."

You have never tried to help yourself, thought Galileo. But, after all, Michelangelo was his brother—and he had made a promise to his father to look after the family. "Well," he said, with a pleasant smile, "we shall see what we can do. Meanwhile, you will live with me, of course."

Michelangelo did not bother to thank Galileo. He said he was hungry and asked for some breakfast. He said he was travel-worn and asked where he could wash. He asked to see his room and said that it was rather small, but that it would do. In short, he behaved in his usual spoiled-little-boy manner. Galileo sighed and shook his head. He knew that Michelangelo would never change, and he suspected that he would go on supporting Michelangelo forever.

During his fourth year at the university, Galileo invented an instrument that was to gain him, for the first time, much money as well as recognition. When the idea first came to him, he was so struck by the possibilities that he made a special trip to Venice to discuss the invention with Brother Sarpi.

"Tell me what you think of this, Paolo. You know, of course, that the ordinary compass now in use to measure distances, or to make circles, consists simply of two legs which are hinged together at the top. Now, supposing the legs of the compass were two flat pieces of metal shaped like a quarter of a circle. I make lines on the legs and on the quadrant crosspiece so—"

Galileo seized a piece of paper on Sarpi's desk and drew rapidly.

"You see, depending on how you set the legs of this compass, you can find the square roots and cube roots of numbers. The different kinds of money to be found in the Italian states can be equalized; a set of proportions can be made to calculate on loans; numbers can be calculated which allow a general to regulate his army formations. In short, by opposing different sets of proportions in the proper places on these compass legs, many, many kinds of useful calculations can be made!"

"But this is a marvelous kind of compass!" exclaimed Sarpi. "We must have a model made at once by a metalworker! No, wait! I have a better idea! I will have enough of them made so that we can send them to scholars and important people all over Europe!"

"I'm afraid I can't afford so many—"

"Don't worry about the money! Leave all the details to me. Come, I know a fine engraver who will be able to design your compass for us. One moment, though; we should have a name for it."

"I call it my Geometrical and Military Compass—"

"Excellent!" interrupted Sarpi. "There's nothing as eye-catching as the word 'military.' Also, I think you should prepare a written set of directions on its use."

Galileo's compass was received with great acclaim by kings, generals, engineers, and teachers in Italy, France, and Germany. He began to get orders in the mail for the compass. Men came from the far corners of Europe to receive personal instruction in the use of the compass from its inventor. After estimating the cost of making the instrument, Galileo and Sarpi decided upon a price of fifty florins for each compass. Money began to roll in. Since Sarpi refused to take any of the profits, Galileo soon found his income considerably increased.

The first thing he did was to move into a house which was much larger and had a beautiful garden. The rent was higher than he could afford, so he began taking in student boarders. This meant that he had to have a cook and housekeeper. After a year had passed, he was receiving so many orders for the Geometrical and Military Compass that he hired a metalworker to come and live in his house. Two rooms in the rear of the house were set up as a factory where the compasses were turned out. Now Galileo was selling a copper compass for thirty florins and a silver compass for fifty florins.

With all this money pouring in, from private pupils and the sale of the compass, it seemed that Galileo would soon become a rich man. In 1599, his salary was increased to three hundred and twenty florins. Sagredo and Pinelli had badgered the Riformatori into granting this increase. "Do you want Venice to lose the world's greatest scientist and inventor to some other university?" they argued.

Galileo was supremely happy. He ate well, slept well (except for an occasional twinge in his joints on a damp night), and enjoyed the company of his good friends. Often, Galileo would sit under a tree in his garden, surrounded by his pupils, playing his lute for them or discussing the latest books and paintings. He had become a renowned scholar, and young people who had a burning desire to learn science swarmed to Padua to study under the master.

As fast as it came in, however, Galileo's money seemed to melt away. Though he tried to keep accurate accounts in a large book, he was too generous. He overpaid his servants and bought only the best of food to serve his student boarders. He gave lavish gifts to his friends. He sent large sums to Madam Giulia and Livia in Florence. Michelangelo, who had accomplished little in Padua, managed to make many florins disappear into thin air. Galileo found that, in spite of having made some small payments, Virginia's dowry had not yet been paid. Her husband threatened to sue Galileo for the money, an action he could take under the existing laws. Galileo begged for a little time, and promised to see that the debt was paid.

The year was 1600. A new century had come, and with it the whole world began to stir uneasily. Spain had been the country of greatest military power. But in 1588, her entire navy had been destroyed during a war against England. France came to life, and began to build a great new army, equipped with the latest kinds of guns and war machines. England and Holland became two of the greatest sea powers in the world. English ships began to sail across the huge Atlantic Ocean to the New World. Dutch vessels voyaged to the East, to find new riches in India and the East Indies.

Important changes were also taking place in people's minds. A great division had occurred in the religious thinking of Europe. Though most of Europe was broken into many separate little political states, reigned over by kings, princes, and dukes, there had always been a single form of Christianity. The leader of the religious thought of the people lived in Rome, capital city of the Italian Papal State. Besides influencing religious thinking, this leader, who was called the Pope, exerted much political influence over all the countries and states.

In the year 1517, a German monk named Martin Luther began a movement that sought to change some of the religious ideas of the leader in Rome. Since Luther claimed to be protesting against the Papal State, he and his followers were called Protestants. Many princes and kings of small European states, particularly in Germany, joined his movement. By 1600, the Protestants had become a powerful and important influence in world affairs.

It was a strange time. In many cases, a person's religious thinking depended on where he lived. If he lived in a country governed by a prince who favored Protestantism, he became a Protestant. If the prince changed his mind and returned to the fold of the Papal State, the chances were that his people did the same.

The leaders in Rome considered the Protestant revolt to be a terrible heresy. They attempted to fight this revolt against their religious and political authority. One of their weapons was an organization called the Inquisition. Every large city in countries faithful to Rome had a man appointed as Chief Inquisitor. His job was to search out people opposed to the religious ideas authorized by the papal authorities. Such people, when found, were put in prison, questioned, often tortured, and put on trial. In many cases, their lives were at stake.

It was in the first year of this new century that Galileo became aware of the power of the Inquisition. A greatly disturbed Sarpi came to him on a bleak day in February.

"Galileo, you remember the case of that wandering monk, Giordano Bruno? He was that odd fellow who traveled all the way to England and back and was arrested seven years ago by the Inquisition."

Galileo thought for a moment. "Oh, yes. Wasn't he accused of saying dreadful things against the authorities at Rome?"

Sarpi's mouth spread in a thin, humorless smile. "He was accused of interpreting the Copernican astronomy in a heretical way! He was accused of spreading the idea that if the planets moved around the sun, as Copernicus said, then there could be other suns and other earths revolving about them in the heavens. He taught that the earth was not the only body of its kind placed in the center of the whole universe, as Aristotle holds."

"I can't understand why the people at Rome should get so excited about that! After all, to discover the truth about nature a scientist must make all kinds of guesses."

"Listen to me, Galileo! This is not a trivial affair! Bruno was burned at the stake by the Inquisition in Rome last week! I just had the news from the papal ambassador at Venice!"

"Burned? But that's a terrible thing! Why should a man be punished for his scientific ideas?"

"You are not aware of what is happening in the world outside your university, Galileo! There are men at Rome who are afraid that their power will be taken from them. They fear change—any kind of change that might make people think differently. Can't you see? The writings of Aristotle have become part of the world's religious beliefs. Any contradiction of Aristotle means a change in thinking—whether it has anything to do with religion or not. The way the men in Rome would have it, to say that Aristotle is wrong about anything is like saying that the word of God in the Bible is wrong!"

"I never heard such nonsense! I go to church regularly. I certainly believe in God devoutly. But I know that some of Aristotle's scientific ideas are completely wrong! Now, what has one thing to do with the other?"

"I agree! Such things are obvious to intelligent men like you and myself. But the men responsible for Bruno's death will stop at nothing, I am afraid, to keep people from believing that the sun is the center of the world and that the earth moves. I am well acquainted with their methods. Lately, I have used my political prestige to keep them from becoming powerful in Venice. They have begun to plot against me. I have been warned that they plan to have me killed!"

"Why should such ruthless and stupid men have power over people's lives?" The one thing that could make Galileo angry was stupidity and ignorance. "Do these Inquisitors hope to stop the advance of science by their actions? They ought to know that it never can be done, no matter how hard they try!"

"Nevertheless, Galileo, I really came to Padua to warn you. Don't argue so openly against the Aristotelian system of the universe in your lectures. If you must talk about Copernican astronomy, discuss the whole business as though it were a mathematical exercise."

"As you know very well, Paolo, that's the only way I can talk about it. There is really no concrete evidence that the sun is the center of the world, or that the earth revolves. Oh, if I could only get out there in the sky and look down at the whole universe!"

"Heaven is where you may wind up, if the Inquisition gets hold of you! Remember Bruno! Please, Galileo, promise you'll take my advice!"

"Haven't I always taken your good advice? I'll be careful, don't worry. Now, come into the dining room. The cook put a delicious lamb roast on this morning—smell it? Mmmmm! I'll wager it's just about done! And while we let it melt in our mouths, I'll tell you about an idea I have for a way of measuring heat."

"Something new? Lord, with you it's one thing after another—" Sarpi followed Galileo into the room where hungry students were already beginning to gather about the huge oval table.

As they sat down to eat, Michelangelo appeared. "Just in time, brother," called Galileo. "Sit down and have dinner with us."

"Who's hungry!" cried Michelangelo. "I have other fish to fry today!" He walked over to where Galileo and Sarpi sat. Galileo could see that he was quite excited.

"What is it, Michelangelo?" Galileo knew that his brother never missed a free meal unless he was ill.

"I have found a patron, a very rich prince!"

"Well, that's wonderful! Who is this patron?"

"A prince from Poland. I can hardly pronounce his name, but he is wealthy beyond measure! I am to join his court, where I will share his table. I will have my own servants to wait upon me. I will be given a coach and horses for my own use. Best of all, my salary, as court musician, will be three hundred florins a year!"

"Congratulations!" Turning to Sarpi, Galileo asked proudly, "Didn't I say that Michelangelo's talent would be recognized some day?"

Sarpi, who knew how much of a millstone Michelangelo had been about his generous brother's neck, smiled and said nothing.

"Well!" Galileo rose and clapped Michelangelo on the back. "When do you begin as musician to this prince?"

"That's what I wanted to see you about. I have to travel to Poland myself to join the court. And I thought—" Michelangelo paused and looked at Brother Sarpi. "Perhaps we'd better talk about it alone."

"Why? Paolo is one of the family. Out with it!"

"I promise I will pay it all back—and more! I need some traveling clothes and some cash. About five hundred florins will cover my expenses."

"Five hundred florins! That's a lot of money! Don't forget, I just promised Mother that I would pay eight hundred florins of Livia's dowry. Her fiancé won't marry her unless the family pays him eighteen hundred florins all told."

"Look here, this is my one chance, Galileo! I'll make good in Poland, I know I will! I swear to you I will not only pay you every cent of the five hundred florins, but I'll help pay Livia's dowry. I'll pay half—nine hundred florins—I give you my word!"

Galileo sighed. He could not bring himself to deny Michelangelo his first great opportunity. "Very well. Come to my study and I will give you the money."

He and Michelangelo left the room, while Brother Sarpi and the students looked at one another and shook their heads. Their poor Galileo was helpless in the clutches of a brother who took everything and gave nothing. They would all have been ready and willing to throw Michelangelo out of the house in a moment. But they did not wish to hurt the feelings of the great man they loved.

A few days later, Michelangelo departed for Poland. He bade Galileo a fond farewell, but was careful not to mention his promise to contribute to Livia's dowry. Not a person in the house was sorry to see him go.

Galileo returned to his work and the lecture hall, but said less about Copernican astronomy. He worked out the details of his new invention, an instrument which measured degrees of hot and cold. One day, while thinking about why heat and cold had never been measured mathematically, Galileo realized that the only instrument actually used by man to tell hot from cold was the human nervous system. A man dipped his finger into water to tell if it were warm or cold. But this allowed him only to determine the difference between such extremes as very hot, lukewarm, cool, and very cold. Galileo felt that there should be a way to measure how hot something was in terms of numbers. Thus, small changes in temperature could be noted. He realized that the human senses could often be deceived, and were not to be trusted. A piece of ice, held against the skin, could cause a sensation of heat and burning.

Gradually, the idea for a temperature-measuring instrument took form. He had the glassblower at the university make him a thin tube of glass. The hollow part was not much thicker than a blade of grass. This tube was welded at one end on to a hollow glass bulb. Galileo knew that when air was heated, it expanded. He found that if he warmed the bulb in the palm of his hand for a few moments and then plunged the open end of the tube into a bowl of water, the water would rise up into the tube to a certain height.

With the tube in the water this way, any change in the temperature of the bulb would make the column of water in the tube go up or down. If the bulb became warmer, the expanding air forced the water down. Chilling the bulb caused the auto contract, and the column of water grew higher. He made scratches on the outside of the tube to mark heights of the water column for very hot and very cold. Just as he had done with the Pulsilogia, he marked off equal intervals between these two scratches. Now he had a way of measuring small changes in temperature.

He did not spend much time improving this instrument. Instead, he became interested in something entirely new.

Pinelli had just purchased a new book which had come all the way from England. Its title was *On a Magnet,* and it had been written by Sir William Gilbert, a man who was physician to Queen Elizabeth of England. The subject of the strange rocks, called lodestones, which always turned one end to the north and the other to the south fascinated Galileo.

But he did not concentrate on this subject very long. In October of the year 1604, a new star appeared in the heavens over Padua. There was terror among the people. What did this signify? The star was so bright, it stood out from all the rest. Night after night, it appeared in the same spot. Some self-styled magicians predicted that it meant a new horrible war was coming. Others said that there would be a new outbreak of the plague. Astrologers were convinced that the end of the world was near.

The Aristotelian scientists were also horrified by the appearance of the star, but for other reasons. According to Aristotle, the heavens out beyond the sphere of the moon could never change. All was perfect there—nothing new could appear in the sky. And yet, here was this great light in the sky, night after night, where, a short while ago, there had been no star.

All the learned men of Venice and Padua waited to hear what these scientists would have to say about the star. Their explanation soon came. Since the star catalogues, which contained the names and positions of all known stars in the sky, did not mention this particular shining body, it could not be a star. And since Aristotle had said that nothing could ever change beyond the sphere of the moon, the so-called star was an optical illusion. It simply was not there. Perhaps it was the reflection of the sun bouncing off the moon, nothing more. After all, Aristotle could not be wrong.

Galileo observed the strange new light in the heavens night after night. Since the light did not change its position with respect to the stars nearest it, he decided that it was really a star. When he was ready, he lectured on the new star in the Aula Magna of the university. Those who came in time were able to crowd into the hall, elbow to elbow. Hundreds were left standing outside the doors, which were left open so they could hear.

The Aristotelians were wrong, declared Galileo boldly. This was too far away to be in the sphere of the moon. This was a new star, which could be called new only because, for some reason, its inner fires had just broken through its surface. He predicted that the star would soon burn itself out and would become invisible again. The star had always been in that spot in the heavens, and would continue to be there long after it had become invisible.

Galileo's lecture caused a great scandal in the university. There had been very little trouble between him and the Aristotelian professors. But now he had challenged the followers of Aristotle. Professor Cremonini, the leading advocate of Aristotle's ideas at Padua, said with disdain that Galileo's argument was sheer nonsense. He proceeded to quote from all the books ever written on astronomy by followers of Aristotle. If all these famous scholars agreed that there could be no new appearing and disappearing stars in the sky, why, then, how could Galileo dare to call them all liars? Obviously, Professor Galilei didn't know what he was talking about.

Aristotelian scientists in other Italian universities, hearing about the contest, backed up their champion, Cremonini. They published little booklets in which they wrote venomous arguments against Galileo's lectures. Some of the religious leaders declared that the new heavenly body had been created by God to remind man of His power. Most of them, however, sided with Cremonini against Galileo.

Eighteen months later, the star disappeared and was seen no more. The world did not end, and none of the magical prophecies came to pass. The people of Padua forgot about the whole thing. But there were some who remembered the star with bitterness—the Aristotelian professors. The new star had left its mark. For the first time, Galileo had enemies who hated him beyond measure.

Chapter VIII

Shortly after classes had ended for the summer, Galileo was invited to spend a few weeks as the guest of his friend Sagredo. The invitation was appealing, for Padua was a hot inland city in the summer. Venice, however, was cooled by the breezes of the Adriatic Sea.

Galileo was enjoying a leisurely lunch on a little outdoor terrace, when Sagredo appeared. There was a look of excitement on his face. "Ah, here you are, Galileo. I just heard the most astounding news!"

"It must have been astounding to make you late for lunch!"

"I heard about a new scientific invention this morning. It is reported that a lens grinder in Holland has invented a kind of instrument called a spyglass. It can be used to see objects at a great distance."

"How did you come to hear about this spyglass?"

"I was at Sarpi's home this morning for a few moments. Some of his friends were there. Everyone was talking about it! This Dutchman gave the Count of Nassau one of those spyglasses as a present. The Count has told people that he can see objects which are two miles away as clearly as though they were right in front of his eyes!"

"Describe this spyglass to me."

"From what I heard, it seems to be simply a tube with a glass lens fixed at each end. You hold it up to your eye and—presto!—the distant becomes the near!"

"A lens fixed at each end—" Galileo sat for a moment, deep in thought. Meanwhile, Sagredo called to a passing servant to bring him some lunch. "Have you ever heard of such an instrument?" he asked, as he sat down opposite Galileo.

"No," murmured Galileo, "never." Suddenly he sat up, his eyes sparked by a new interest. "But there's no reason why I can't make one. In fact, there's no reason why I can't make a *better* one! It's only a question of optical geometry and the laws of perspective. Let me fetch some paper and a pencil."

"I'll call for some—" Sagredo began, but Galileo, too impatient to wait for a servant, had already run indoors. In a moment, he returned and began to sketch some diagrams, explaining to Sagredo as he drew.

"Now, this Hollander must have just held the lenses out and moved them back and forth, until he got a sharp image. But after all, Sagredo, men's eyes differ. There should be a way of changing the focus of the lenses. Suppose I make two tubes instead of one and have them fitted so that one will slide smoothly inside the other. Now, with a lens at each end, I could push the smaller tube in or pull it out, depending on what the position is for my eyes to see a sharp image."

"What I don't quite understand is how such an image appears," put in Sagredo.

"Oh, I would have to give you a whole series of lectures on the geometry of light to make that clear!" Nevertheless, Galileo tried to show Sagredo in a simple way how a ray of light, traveling in a straight line, was bent by a lens. If light rays came from a distant object to a lens whose sides were bowed outward—a convex lens—the rays were bent so as to form an upside-down image of that object. But if one were to let the light coming through the convex lens come through a lens whose sides were curved in—a concave lens—then the upside-down image would appear right side up and much nearer.

"Therefore, by changing the curve of the lenses, it should be possible to make a spyglass to see vast distances! It won't take me long to calculate how to make an instrument that will make objects at a distance of nine miles appear as though they were only one mile away." And while Sagredo, protesting that he was too excited to eat, nibbled at his food and watched, Galileo began to draw optical designs on the paper.

A few moments later, his pen stopped moving. "There, my spyglass is finished." He made some rapid calculations on the margin of the paper. "This spyglass should bring objects that are over nine miles away close to the eye of the observer."

Galileo rose. "Sagredo, many thanks for these few days of pleasure and comfort. But I must return to Padua today."

"Today? But you have hardly begun your visit—"

"I know, and I promise I shall return. But I have to finish what I have begun here. I am determined to perfect the instrument that this Dutchman stumbled upon. It's just a question of calculating the proper curvature for the glass lenses. Why, there may be no end to how far one may be able to see with such a spyglass!"

Back at his home in Padua, Galileo began to spend the days and nights in the workshop rooms with his compass-making craftsman. He ground glass block after glass block into fat, curved lenses. The work was exacting and arduous. Often, after an afternoon spent patiently rotating the grinding powder over the glass surface, his joints were on fire with burning pain. But Galileo only gritted his teeth and kept on with the monotonous task.

At length, the lenses were done. His metalworker had fashioned two hollow tubes, one of which fitted inside the other. A large convex lens went into the open end of the larger tube, while a small concave lens was cemented into the open end of the small tube. Galileo climbed to the roof of his house with the instrument. Placing the end of the small tube to his eye, he pushed the tubes together slowly, until the blur he saw became a sharp picture. It was a tree. Galileo put the spyglass down and looked in the direction in which it had been pointed. He could see no tree—only the distant horizon, a wavy black line far beyond the roofs of Padua. He exclaimed with joy. His spyglass was a success!

He went straight to Pinelli with his new invention. Galileo's friend was first puzzled, and then filled with amazement when he looked through the long tube. "How far I can see with this!" he exclaimed.

"You inspire me to name the instrument!" cried Galileo. "I have been trying to think of a better name than spyglass. But the words 'see far' have given me an idea. The Greek word for far is *tele,* and the word for see is *scopein.* I shall call this a *telescope!*"

"A scholarly name for such a wonderful instrument," agreed Pinelli. "Listen," he continued, "I see an opportunity for you to establish yourself permanently in the hearts of the leading citizens of Venice. How long will it take you to make another like this?"

"Now that I have the dimensions calculated—only about three weeks."

"Good. Make another. Have your engraver make a very fancy tube, with the arms of the Republic of Venice engraved upon it. Then we shall take it with us to Venice. We shall allow the Doge and his Senate to look through the telescope. Then, you will present it to them with your compliments."

Galileo knew that his greatest rewards had come from following the advice of his good friends. He agreed to begin work on the second telescope immediately. On the twentieth of August, he and Pinelli set forth for Venice.

Saint Mark's Square was filled with a curious crowd on the following day. The rumor had already spread that the great Master Galileo was going to reveal a scientific miracle to the leader of the Venetian Republic, Doge Leonardo Donate. High atop the Tower of the Clock stood the famous Two Moors of Venice. These were two great statues, one on each side of a huge bell. Each figure had a hammer in its hand. Exactly on the hour, a whirring mechanism made these Moors turn and strike the time on the bell with their hammers.

Even as the Moors began to turn and clang out the noon hour, a troop of soldiers in dress-parade uniform marched out of the Doge's palace into the square. Forming a double file, they pushed back the people until a long narrow passage had been cleared from the palace to the campanile. As soon as this had been done, a group of finely dressed nobles filed slowly from the Doge's palace. They formed themselves into a kind of procession, and the crowd made room for them as they moved toward the Campanile of Saint Mark—the bell tower that stretched over three hundred feet up into the sky.

First came the Doge and his wife, clad in the splendid clothes that befitted their rank. Though it was a warm day, the Doge wore an ermine cape over a robe of rich red velvet. He was an old man, with a flowing white beard, and he moved slowly. By his side tottered the Dogessa, his wife, on her elevated shoes. Her dress was of elegant yellow silk embroidered all over with red lilies. About her wrinkled neck hung strands of lustrous pearls, and in her hair she wore a jeweled tiara that sparkled in the sun.

Behind the Doge and his wife came Galileo, bearing his telescope, accompanied by Pinelli and Brother Sarpi. After Galileo and his party marched the six councilors of the Doge. They were clad in scarlet robes and hats, and their faces were solemn and wrinkled. They were followed by the Council of Ten, who, like judges of a supreme court, made decisions regarding the application of laws. Their robes were deep purple in color. Completing the long procession were the sixty members of the Venetian Senate, shuffling forward slowly in their black robes.

The people standing behind the lines of soldiers on each side of the procession tried to press closer when Galileo passed by. Fingers pointed at the long tube of the telescope in his hand, and mouths were open with wonder and fear. A little boy, whose head projected from between the sturdy legs of a soldier, reached up and tugged at Galileo's robe. With a smile, Galileo turned and patted the tousled head. The small boy did not know who the bearded man in the velvet robe was, nor did he have any idea of what was taking place that day. He only loved to watch parades of all kinds. But years later, he was to tell his grandchildren many times of how the great Master Galileo had reached out to touch him.

At the entrance to the campanile, the Doge turned and signified that his councilors should be the first to accompany him and Galileo to the top of the tower. The rest of the legislators would have to await their turn, since there was room for only a few people at the top of the tower. There were no steps inside the campanile. Instead, the architect had constructed a ramp that spiraled its way to the top. Henry II, King of France, on a visit to Venice in 1574, had ridden a horse to the very top of the tower to demonstrate his remarkable ability in the saddle.

Slowly, because of their age, the Doge and his wife, followed by the councilors, ascended the ramp. Galileo and his friends followed at a respectful distance. Every few moments, the noble elders had to pause for breath. A dim light filtered into the tower from the oblong slots in the brickwork. The air was damp and somewhat fetid.

It was with obvious relief that the party reached the open balcony at the top of the campanile. Over them, in two rows, hung the gleaming bells that were rung from the ground floor by ropes. On the observation platform stood the official lookout, who watched for merchant ships coming into Venice. From his vantage point, three hundred feet up, he could see the sails of an incoming ship long before they were visible to watchers on shore. Most important, of course, he would be able to spot an attacking enemy fleet and to sound the alarm.

While the Doge and his followers were resting, Galileo put the telescope to his eye and gazed out to sea. Then he turned and asked the lookout, "Your pardon, my good fellow, but is there a vessel upon the horizon?"

The man shaded his eyes from the sun's glare and stared at the far line where the sky met the water. "No, Your Excellence, I can see nothing on the horizon—not even a cloud."

Galileo smiled and turned to the Doge. "Here is a man with keen vision who can see no ship approaching. However, Your Worship, if you will kindly put my telescope to your right eye and close the other, I believe you will see something interesting over there, to the southeast."

The Doge did as he was told with trembling hands. As he swung the telescope a little to the right, he gasped, "I see something! Something!"

"What do you see, Your Worship?" asked Galileo.

"It's not quite clear."

"Try pushing the smaller tube in a little. If that doesn't help, pull it out a bit. Now, is that better?"

"A ship! I see a ship! It's heading under full sail for the harbor!"

The Dogessa and the councilors strained their eyes in the direction indicated by the Doge. They saw only the vague line of the horizon.

"Wait! Wait!" The excitement of the Doge was higher than before. "I can see her flag! Why, it's one of our navy galleys! I can see the oar deck quite clearly. It's the *Dolphina*, back from Trieste!"

He said no more, for the impatient Dogessa had snatched the telescope from his eye and had placed it to her own. When she had exclaimed over the miracle, the telescope was passed from one councilor to the other.

The Doge asked for the telescope again, and amused himself for a half hour looking at different parts of the city. He called out a running description of what he saw to the others.

"Oho, there are two gondoliers having a fight near the Bridge of Saint Rocco! Splash! There goes one into the water! And look, I can see the glass factory on the Island of Murano as though it were next door! There goes a little boy into a candy shop! What a marvelous thing this telescope is!"

For another hour and one half, the Doge, his wife, and the six councilors passed the telescope from hand to hand, chattering with excitement about the distant scenes that came before their astonished eyes. The Dogessa declared all in one breath that it was one of the greatest miracles that had ever come to pass in Venice, that she had to have one of these new playthings or she would die, and that she would spend years just looking through Professor Galilei's invention. The councilors tried for a while to appear grave and dignified, but soon they were gabbling away as excitedly as the Dogessa.

Finally, Pinelli coughed discreetly and reminded the Doge that there were others below waiting to look through Galileo's telescope. Sarpi broke in to point out that the *Dolphina* was now visible as a tiny speck on the horizon. The Doge and his company began to descend the ramp, chattering enthusiastically among themselves about the wonder they had just seen.

It took the better part of an afternoon for the whole delegation to climb, look through the telescope, and descend from the tower. When the last amazed senator had left, Pinelli danced a little jig and gave Galileo a hearty thump on the back.

"Oho! Did you see their faces? What a success! But come, let us go down. There's still work to be done. We have to compose a letter to the Doge which you will present to him at an audience tomorrow."

"We do? I will?" Galileo looked confused.

"Little details which I forgot to mention. Come, we'll sup at Paolo's house and then work on the letter."

"I'm sorry for one thing." Galileo shook his head sadly. "I wish Sagredo could have been here to share this moment with us."

"I know," said Brother Sarpi. "But the orders of the Foreign Office cannot be disobeyed. If he could have put off his voyage for only two weeks! But right now, he is somewhere on the Adriatic Sea on a mission to the East. Perhaps if we had a telescope large enough, we could see him!"

The other two laughed. "Some day there will be such a telescope," prophesied Galileo.

As the three emerged from the doorway of the bell tower, they were greeted by a roar of acclaim from the crowd. The members of the Senate had spoken freely of the wonderful things they had witnessed, and the story of the amazing telescope had spread like wildfire through the massed citizens of Venice. They pressed close to Galileo, those nearest trying to touch his clothing and the telescope, shouting hoarse approval. The formation of soldiers finally managed to force a path through the crowd, so that Galileo and his friends could cross the square safely.

The following afternoon, the two Moors were striking the hour of three with their hammers when Galileo, Pinelli, and Sarpi were ushered into the hallway of the Doge's palace. The walls were hung with paintings by famous Venetian artists. In little niches around the walls stood polished suits of armor mounted on marble pedestals. The floor was made of blocks of multicolored marble, rubbed to a mirror finish.

"We shall see you after the ceremony," murmured Pinelli in Galileo's ear. Fumbling nervously with the telescope and the letter, Galileo followed the usher who had met him at the gates. They came to a pair of great doors whose panels were inlaid with burnished gold. Two footmen, dressed in handsome scarlet jackets and white hose, slowly swung the doors open. Galileo found himself alone, walking into the great Council Hall.

Before him, at what seemed to be a long distance, sat the Doge. Behind the leader sat the members of the Council and the Senate, in a great semicircle. The rest of the hall was crowded with noblemen and ladies who had been allowed to attend the ceremony. As Galileo walked between the two rows of nodding and whispering people, he imagined he saw Pinelli, smiling and waving him on. Seeing that familiar face reassured him.

He knelt before the Doge, presented the telescope and the letter, and made the little speech he had been practicing all morning. The old leader, obviously delighted to have the instrument, nodded his head in vigorous approval. All the people present broke into loud applause. The Doge made a sign for silence.

"Procurator Prioli will read our pronouncement," he declared.

Galileo pricked up his ears. The Procurator was one of the top officials of the University of Padua.

Signer Prioli was a tall man, with a huge frame. Even with his velvet cloak of office and flat cap, he gave the impression of being an athlete, rather than a man of scholarship. He smiled at Galileo and began to read.

"Master Galileo Galilei, having been mathematical lecturer in Padua for seventeen years, to the gain of the university, and to the satisfaction of all; and having made known to the world during his professorship many great discoveries and inventions; and having now invented an instrument, known as the telescope, by which things which are most distant can be brought within easy sight, and which may be useful to us in many different ways; it is proper that this Council gratefully recognize his genius and great labors for the good of all the people by electing him to the professorship of mathematics at Padua for the rest of his life. Secondly, in consideration of all that has been said above, his salary shall be one thousand florins a year, said salary to begin as of this date, the twenty-fifth of August, 1609."

Applause broke out, louder than before. The Doge and his councilors signed the parchment, and the ceremony was over. The Doge retired to his private rooms, fondling the telescope like a little boy who has been given a new toy. The

people in the hall closed in about Galileo, shaking his hand and congratulating him.

"How useful your telescope will be for observing the enemy's movements in time of war!" exclaimed a general, wringing Galileo's hand.

"And for knowing hours earlier that our ships have returned from their voyages safe and sound," added a merchant.

"Very handy for locating wild game during a hunt," said a nobleman.

"One's private life will never be safe again!" giggled a Venetian lady, pursing her lips, which were painted with red cosmetic.

Bowing, nodding, thanking them all, Galileo made his way out to the doorway, where Pinelli and Sarpi helped him escape.

"Well," asked Pinelli, "what do you think now?"

"I—I don't know what to say!"

"It's only what you deserve!" Pinelli and Sarpi each embraced Galileo and gave him congratulatory kisses on the cheek.

"And now," said Galileo, disengaging himself from their embrace, "I must return to Padua."

"What? At this moment? Why, we had planned a celebration—"

"Some other time, dear friends. But I must return to some work I left behind. Believe me, if it were not urgent, I would gladly stay here with you."

Reluctantly his friends watched him go.

Back in his house, Galileo sat in the study and pondered. He had no unfinished work to do in Padua—he had made that excuse just to get away. He did not know why he had not wanted to remain in Venice, except that something about the Doge's reception still bothered him.

A useful invention, he said to himself, but useful for what? To fight wars? To see ships at sea? To hunt wild boars? It seemed that his telescope should serve a loftier purpose.

He thought about the geometry of light rays, and how he had explained it to Sagredo. "If light rays come from a distant object to a lens—" How distant could the object be? Could it be, he asked himself, as distant as the stars?

And suddenly he knew the answer. Why not point his telescope at the most distant things there were—the stars themselves! Were there secrets of nature hidden there in the heavens that the telescope would reveal? He ran to the window and looked up at the sky. It was cloudless. The sun was moving near the western horizon; in an hour or so, it would be setting. Impatient for night to fall, Galileo ran to his workshop and began cleaning the lenses of his telescope.

The red rim of the sun was just sinking below the horizon when Galileo made his way to the roof of his house. It was still too light for any stars to be visible. While he waited, he fussed with the instrument, looking at the corner of a distant house, or at the branch of a tree on the horizon. Finally the shadowy dusk became deep blue night, and the stars could be seen twinkling above.

He put the telescope to his eye and tried to focus on one of the bright stars in the familiar constellation of the Big Dipper. The telescope did not seem to work correctly.

Finally when he had pushed the smaller tube with the eyepiece lens as far forward as it could go, he saw a little bright spot of light. Could this little pin point of light be the same as that wide twinkling star seen without the telescope? He turned the instrument on another star, and again saw only a little point of light.

As he looked at the star, it began to dance up and down, until it became a blur before his eyes. Do the stars vibrate? he asked himself. Then he realized that it was his own hand that was causing the telescope to shake. Even though his hands seemed steady enough, the slightest quiver caused the telescope's field of vision to shake enormously. He made a note to have his metalworker construct a stand for the telescope the very next day.

Suddenly he noticed that the moon had risen—a bright full moon. How familiar that yellow circle of light was to him! He had studied its face for many nights. He knew all the shadowy and light spots on that yellow marble in the sky. But always he had looked only with his unaided eyes. What would he see when he looked at the moon through the telescope?

He was not prepared for what he saw. In his surprise, the telescope almost dropped from his hands. He waited a moment until his hands were steady once more and looked at the moon again. It was unbelievable!

Gone was the appearance of polished smoothness. He was looking at the surface of a marble dotted with little eruptions, like craters of volcanoes. Why, even their shadows were visible! There were mountains on the moon, just as there were on earth! And he was the first man on earth who had ever seen them!

Now he had another unshakable argument against the Aristotelian astronomers. Aristotle claimed that the moon, like all heavenly bodies, had a surface that was smooth and perfect. There were many theories to explain the light and dark spots on the moon. One was that the dark shadows that were visible to the naked eye were only the result of interference with the moon's light by vapors rising from the earth.

But now Galileo had proof that the moon was a body very much like the earth, and that the surface of the moon was reflecting the light of the sun. The light parts of the moon, he decided, were high land surfaces; the dark areas, the oceans.

Soon his eyes tired, and all he could see was a blur. Reluctantly, he left the roof, but not until he had taken a long last look at the night sky. There were secrets to be discovered among those blinking little lights up there! And he, Galileo, would find them and make them known!

Was the earth the center of the world? Or was it the sun? He knew now that his telescope would point the way to the truth.

Chapter IX

After a few nights of observation, Galileo decided that his present telescope was far too small. In order to make accurate observations of the moon and its surface, he would have to design and build a telescope that would bring the moon closer to his eyes. Without wasting a moment, he began to calculate the curvature of lenses that would bring the moon twenty times nearer to the earth.

Now that he had learned the technique of lens grinding, it took him only a few weeks to prepare this telescope. To keep the instrument from vibrating, he devised an iron stand. The telescope was fixed firmly to the stand by a swivel which allowed him to point the lens in any direction.

But it took only one night of observation to show him that the new telescope was still not large enough. He spent weeks calculating a set of lenses that would bring the moon thirty times nearer to the earth. Meanwhile, he sent one of his other telescopes to the new Grand Duke of Tuscany, Cosimo de Medici the Second. Pinelli asked Galileo why he had favored the Tuscan ruler in this way.

Galileo looked abashed. "To tell you the truth, Pinelli, I still dream about going back to my native country one of these days."

"Haven't you been happy in Venice?"

"You know I have! A man couldn't be happier with such good friends and a wonderful position for the rest of his life. But sometimes I think back to the old days in my native city of Florence. I miss the thousand and one ways in which Tuscany is different from Venice. There's no good reason I can give. It's just that Florence will always seem like home to me."

Pinelli had been understanding. He changed the subject quickly. Just the thought of Galileo's leaving Padua made him feel very sad.

It was October, and Galileo's work at the university began anew. His time was taken up with new lectures, new pupils, and the many details that were part of a professor's life. The Council of the Doge asked him to help with the plans of a new water viaduct to the hills near the city of Venice. Work on the new telescope went slowly. Galileo spoke of it to few people. He was not quite sure whether he would be able to focus the new lenses he was grinding.

Finally, just after the New Year, the telescope was completed. Now Galileo could not wait to turn the long tube toward the heavens. On the first clear night, he stationed himself on the roof. It was midwinter. Galileo knew he would pay for this night with a miserable ache in his bones for days.

He had invited Brother Sarpi to be with him to share this first night of observing through the new telescope. Sarpi had arrived at dusk with his bodyguard, four soldiers assigned by the Doge to protect the monk. Only three years before, as he had predicted, an attempt had been made on Sarpi's life. He had been left for dead in one of the narrow alleys of Venice with a stiletto in his cheekbone. Fortunately, the wound had not been fatal. Fabrizio had tended him carefully until he had recovered. Some of the conspirators who had plotted to assassinate Brother Sarpi were captured. Before their execution, they admitted that some of the leaders in the Papal State had paid them to commit the crime. Since then, Sarpi had lived in fear of his life, despite the constant presence of his guards.

Slowly Sarpi climbed the ladder that led from a room on the top floor to the flat roof. Two of the guards stationed themselves downstairs in the front hall. The other two, with a sigh of relief, removed their shiny, uncomfortable steel helmets and relaxed at the foot of the ladder.

"Welcome, Paolo. How do you feel tonight? I hope your bones aren't aching the way mine are!"

"Don't forget, Galileo, my bones are older than yours!" He put a sensitive finger to the long scar on his cheek. "This souvenir of the stiletto lets me know when a damp night is coming."

"Enough! We are becoming two whining old men! There's work to be done. See, here is my new beauty, ready for a look at the heavenly mysteries. Well, what shall we observe first?"

Sarpi scanned the sky about him for a moment, and then pointed. "How about the Pleiades?"

Galileo looked up at the constellation of Taurus the Bull. A cluster of six stars gleamed faintly. Galileo laughed. "It has always amused me that they are called the Pleiades, after the name given by the ancient Greeks to the seven daughters of the god Atlas. Yet, there are only six stars visible. Men are so in the habit of accepting ancient authority that they even see things that aren't there!"

"Perhaps we'll find the missing star tonight!" joked Sarpi, as Galileo pointed the telescope at the Pleiades and began to focus the lenses.

"Missing star, did you say?" cried Galileo suddenly. "One missing star?" He began to laugh, as though Sarpi had made a tremendous joke.

"What is it? What do you see?"

"Come look for yourself, Paolo. The daughters of Atlas are not seven, but I'll wager they are almost forty in number!"

Sarpi bent to the eyepiece, adjusted the lens to his eyes, and gasped. "Why, the Pleiades are a whole cloud of stars! This is incredible!"

"You know the old saying, Paolo—seeing is believing. I tell you, there are more stars in the heavens than old Aristotle ever dreamed of. Now, let me look again. I want to sketch the positions of those unseen stars about the six bright ones."

Galileo drew a few sheets of paper from his pocket. As he sketched, Sarpi asked, "Have you thought about the reason stars look so tiny when seen through the telescope? Even the largest star in the Pleiades looked stripped of the diameter it has when seen with the naked eye."

"I have thought about that for some time," Galileo answered, without looking up from his drawing. "I believe that when we look at a star with the naked eye, so much radiance enters the eye that the star seems to be broad and twinkling. That is, the star is surrounded by a false corona of light. But the telescope stops this false radiance from affecting the eye. I have noticed that the darker the sky, the more effect of broadening. In the twilight sky, stars appear much smaller and dimmer."

"But why do all the stars appear to be about the same size in the telescope?"

"That must be because the stars are so far away from the earth that they can be seen only as bright, twinkling spots. Even with the aid of a telescope, we cannot hope to see the round edge of a star. But the planets are nearer. You recall that when I showed Mars to you through the last telescope I made, it appeared to be a bright little round ball."

"Yes, I remember. What you say seems to make sense. But according to the Aristotelian system of the world, all the stars are on a great wheel, and all are the same distance from the earth."

"Now, Paolo, your understanding of science is too advanced for you to believe that nonsense any more. According to Copernicus, the stars are removed enormously from the sun and its planets. Now, if they are all the same distance from the earth, how is it that there are stars which become visible only when seen through my telescope?"

"They could be stars that give too little light."

"Possibly, but I have a better answer. Perhaps they are not so bright because they are too far away for enough light to get from them to our eyes. I believe the stars are spread throughout the heavens at different distances from the earth."

Galileo had finished his drawing. Paolo, who had been searching the sky, said suddenly, "Isn't that Jupiter just above the horizon?"

"You're right! Jupiter is visible tonight. Well, let's see what the planet looks like with this kind of magnification."

Galileo swung the telescope in the direction of the brightly gleaming planet.

"What in the name of—! Sarpi, put your eye to this tube! Maybe my eye is getting tired already. Tell me, what do you see?"

"A little ball—its edges are rather hazy."

"Adjust the lenses, man!"

"Ah, now the edges are sharper. Why, there is something else there! Right next to the planet! I see a spot of light to the left. No, wait! There are two spots of light!"

"So you see them also! I thought for a moment that my eyes—let me look again."

After a moment, Galileo called to Sarpi. "There are three stars, Paolo. Two on the left and one on the right. And what is strange to me is that they fall in a straight line, right across the equator of Jupiter! Oh, well, that arrangement must be an accident. Jupiter must be moving past some fixed stars which are far beyond the planet. But it does look like an odd arrangement, nevertheless."

Then Galileo found a new subject for the telescope, and the three stars around Jupiter were forgotten. "Do you know how many stars are known in the constellation of Orion the Giant?"

"Bayer's star table, published in 1603, lists thirty-seven stars!"

"Bravo!" joked Galileo. "You are now eligible to become a bachelor in astronomy. But joking aside, I have the telescope pointed at Orion's belt of three stars. Look for yourself."

Sarpi squinted and whistled with amazement. Where the naked eye normally saw only three bright stars, there seemed to be more than fifty pin points of light. "It seems that every where you point your telescope new miracles come into view!" Suddenly Sarpi broke into a fit of coughing.

"We have stayed up here too long." Galileo helped Sarpi to the opening where the ladder led back into the house. "I can feel the ache in my shoulders already from the damp night air."

"Fabrizio warned you that the night air was poisonous for you."

"Unfortunately, the stars are invisible in the daytime. If it is to be a contest between my bones and science, I am afraid that science is the winner!"

After a hot drink and some supper beside the roaring fireplace in the dining room, Sarpi left, promising that he would return as often as he could to observe through the telescope. Galileo sat at his desk and began to copy the sketches he had made on the roof into a notebook. The last drawing he had made was of the planet Jupiter, with the three stars about it.

He looked at this drawing for a long time. It was odd that three stars should line themselves up behind Jupiter in such a straight array. He determined to keep watching Jupiter carefully for the next few days.

The following night, when he swept the sky about Jupiter with the telescope, the three stars were no longer where they had been. They were now grouped to the right of Jupiter, and were closer together.

This puzzled him. If Jupiter had moved to the left, then it was moving in the wrong direction! And how could fixed stars change their position and move closer together? It was very strange.

The third night, clouds covered the sky. Galileo waited until midnight, hoping for a break in the cloud cover. Finally he fell asleep in his chair by the fire in his study. In the morning, he ached as though someone had bruised him from head to foot. Fabrizio had left some medicine for him to take when his pains were too intense. He dragged himself over to the cabinet where he kept the medicine and gulped down the prescribed dose. The mixture of drugs had a horrible sour taste that brought tears to his eyes. Slowly Galileo made his way to his bedroom and lay down, waiting for the attack to pass.

That night, he was on the roof again. The sky was clear, and the yellowish glow of Jupiter hung in the night like a pale diamond. He swung the telescope around and focused on the planet. After a moment, he grunted with satisfaction. The sketch he now drew showed the two stars to the left of Jupiter. The star on the right had disappeared!

There could be no doubt in his mind now that these stars were not shining behind Jupiter—they were moving along *with the planet!* These bright dots he had seen were moons—*moons of Jupiter!*—and they were revolving about Jupiter in the same way that the moon revolved about the earth. This discovery was too great for him to keep to himself. He wasted little time getting to Brother Sarpi's house.

"How can you be sure that they are moons and not stars?" asked Sarpi.

"First, they follow Jupiter in its path—they are not fixed as are the other stars. Secondly, then: light disappears when they move into Jupiter's shadow. If they were stars, with their own internal fire, they would continue to be visible. And the fact that Jupiter throws a shadow means that this planet, like all the planets, is illuminated by the light of the sun!"

"But this is a sensational victory for Copernican astronomy! According to Aristotelian astronomers, the planets shine with their own light."

Galileo snorted. "The telescope shows that it is the light of the sun which makes the other planets visible to us on earth. In the same way, it would be the light of the sun reflecting off the earth's surface that would make the earth visible to an observer on Mars! It must be so! I tell you, Paolo, Jupiter with its four moons is like our solar system. These little planets circle Jupiter in exactly the same way all the other planets circle the sun."

"Nevertheless," warned Sarpi, "be careful how you talk to people about it. Your enemies will not be made any happier by these discoveries."

"I can't see how they will be able to deny the evidence they see with their own eyes. I am planning to reveal all my astronomical discoveries to the world very soon in a little book. I am hoping that it will serve to convince even my enemies of the truth."

"Knowing who your enemies are, Galileo, I despair that they will ever be able to see the truth, even if it were plastered right on the ends of their noses!"

Night after night, whenever the skies were clear, Galileo observed the various bodies that moved in the heavens. He examined the moon's surface carefully. From the size of their shadows, he was able to judge the height of some of the mountains on the moon. They were as high as four or five miles—the same as mountains on the earth! He found that the sun's light reflected from the earth's surface often illuminated the dark part of the moon. This was a greenish, eerie light which astronomers had not been able to explain very well. Galileo called this light "earth-shine."

He turned his telescope on the Milky Way. This faint whitish cloud stretching across the night sky had always puzzled the Aristotelian astronomers. There were a thousand different guesses as to what it was. Galileo was astonished to find that the Milky Way was simply a conglomeration of thousands and thousands of stars filling that part of the sky.

"All the disputes," he wrote in his notebook, "which have tormented astronomers for ages are exploded at once by the indisputable evidence of our eyes. We are freed from the meaningless nonsense of wordy arguments. The Milky Way is nothing else but a mass of innumerable stars planted together in clusters."

His book came off the presses in March. Galileo entitled it *A Message from the Stars*. It was his official announcement to the world of the invention of the telescope and what he had seen through it. He wrote about the surface of the moon, the Milky Way, and the many stars to be seen where, to the naked eye, there appeared only empty sky. Most important of all, he wrote about the moons of the planet Jupiter. He had discovered a fourth moon not long after finding the first three.

As fast as men could transport the book—by carriage, by ship, and by horse—copies of *A Message from the Stars* were sold all over Europe. Those scientists who believed in the Copernican system of the world read the book with joy and acclaim. Aristotelian professors read it with bitterness and hate in their hearts. They could not forgive Galileo for exposing as meaningless all the truths in which they believed.

In Padua, the great astronomer Professor Cremonini lectured against *A Message from the Stars,* declaring that everything Galileo had written was a complete lie. How could the Milky Way be made of stars? Would not Aristotle have said so, if it were true? How could the moon have a surface like the earth's? Aristotle and the great astronomers who had followed him said that the moon was smooth and perfect. As for the moons of Jupiter—bah!—that was hardly worth talking about. He quoted book after book to prove that Galileo was wrong.

Galileo set his telescope up in the courtyard of the university and dared Cremonini to come and look for himself. There was the instrument, pointed right at Jupiter.

"What would you rather believe, my dear Professor, what is written in a book or what you see with your own eyes? Come, look at Jupiter through my telescope!"

But Cremonini rudely shouldered Galileo aside and stamped away, muttering abusive words. He only turned his head to bawl at Galileo, "I don't have to look through your devil's invention! If Aristotle said nothing about such moons, then they do not exist!"

The crowd of students and professors who had witnessed this battle between the two astronomers stood aghast. Many of them appreciated Galileo's genius, but Cremonini was an older man with a solid reputation as a scholar. Which of the two was right?

Galileo, looking at the silent group, was amused. "Don't be alarmed," he reassured them. "Perhaps when Cremonini goes to heaven, he will finally see the four moons of Jupiter as he passes by. No doubt he will believe his own eyes then!"

Everyone roared with laughter. Galileo was still able to capture the fancy of a group with his wit, inside the lecture hall or out.

In spite of all the agitation caused by the publication of his book, Galileo had not forgotten his plans to return to Florence. But the one thing he wanted was to be able to go back to his homeland on his own terms. He knew that the most important thing was to have Cosimo de Medici become his patron.

With this in mind, Galileo had dedicated *A Message from the Stars* to the Grand Duke. But feeling that this was not enough, he made another attempt to flatter the ruler of Tuscany. In honor of Cosimo's family name, the Medici, Galileo named the four moons of Jupiter the Medicean Planets.

He followed this gesture with a letter to Belisario Vinta, Secretary of State to the Grand Duke, and already an old friend.

My dear Belisario:

Though I am happy here at the University of Padua and well paid and honored by the Republic of Venice, I yearn to return to my native city of Florence. I could be more productive of new ideas and inventions than I have been. This is because I have to spend too much of my time with matters which interfere with my own scientific studies. So, if I return to Tuscany, it would be on a basis of being able to spend most of my time on my own work, without the nuisance of lecturing or teaching private pupils.

There are many works which I have in mind. These include a great book on the structure of the universe and three books on motion. These last discuss a science I have invented that is so new that its consequences are beyond the wildest imagination. Also there are books on principles of machines, on the nature of light and colors, on sound and speech, on the causes of the tides, and on the movements of animals.

Also, I plan a book that will prove of utmost importance to the military organization of His Highness. This book will teach a soldier whatever mathematics he must know to carry on his art in a scientific way—that is, it will concern itself with the aiming of cannon, the construction of breastworks, the erection of fortifications, and so on. Also, I wish to take some time to determine the periods of the Medicean Planets about Jupiter—that is, the time it takes each planet to circle Jupiter once. This is a very difficult task of calculation.

I shall be pleased to accept the salary you mention, since it is equivalent to what I am earning now at Padua. Only I would like to ask for a small additional amount to pay whatever debts I now have outstanding—particularly the dowries of my sisters.

I would also be most pleased if His Highness would be kind enough to bestow upon me the additional title (besides that of First Mathematician at the University of Pisa) of Philosopher and Mathematician to Himself. I believe it is a title which I deserve and which will not go unmerited. I hope His Highness will have an opportunity to learn much that will interest him from me. I am

Your obedient servant,
Galileo Galilei

The reply to his letter came in June. Vinta reported happily that Galileo's wish had been granted. He could now return to Florence as chief scientist in all Tuscany and under the protection of the Grand Duke himself!

For now the fame of Galileo had increased to heights it had never reached before. Poets everywhere composed odes in honor of his telescope and the Medicean Planets he had discovered. Minstrels in all the great cities of Italy sang the praises of Galileo, the great astronomer, who had revealed new miracles in the heavens.

Only among the Aristotelian astronomers, and among certain people in Rome who feared that this new astronomy would change religious thinking in a disastrous way, were there fear and distrust of Galileo's discoveries. Here and there, certain religious leaders and Aristotelian professors were planning to combine forces against Galileo.

But Galileo knew nothing of this, nor did he care. He was filled with happiness at the thought of returning to Florence as such an important person. If only my father could be there to greet me, he thought. Oh, why hadn't Vincenzio lived to see this successful homecoming!

But the only ones left to greet him when he came to Florence in September were his sisters and their families. Madam Giulia had not lived to see her son return to Tuscany in triumph. Michelangelo was somewhere in Germany. He had acquired a wife and children, and wrote to Galileo only when he needed money.

Galileo felt somewhat guilty about leaving Brother Sarpi, Pinelli, and Sagredo—the men who had been his stanch friends and allies for eighteen years. Yet, his longing for Florence and all the memories of home were stronger than his ties to Venice. In his twenty-eighth year he had left Florence in disgust, feeling that he was disliked and unwanted. Now, at the age of forty-six, he was returning like a conquering Caesar. He looked forward to nothing but continued happiness and success.

It might have dimmed his happiness, perhaps, if he had heard what Sagredo said upon his return to Venice from the East. When Sagredo landed, some months after Galileo had gone, and learned of what had happened, he became very sad.

"Why did our good friend Galileo leave this free soil?" he asked Sarpi. "Here he had such liberty to speak his mind. He should never have gone back. I am afraid that he will find the Tuscan Court and the University of Pisa filled with envious people who will seek to destroy him if they can!"

Chapter X

Galileo had been settled in his new house in Florence only a short time when he announced two new astronomical discoveries to the world.

First, he had observed Saturn, the outermost planet in the sky, through his telescope, and had found that Saturn, like Jupiter, was not alone. The planet appeared to have a little body on each side, like two ears sticking out. Galileo drew a picture of the strange sight in his notebook.

A few nights later, he observed that the ears seemed to fill out a bit on each side of the planet.

Finally, they reappeared as before.

Here again was evidence that Aristotelian astronomy was wrong. The ideas that nothing new could appear in the heavens and that the planets were all perfectly smooth round bodies were worthless. For here was Saturn with two moons accompanying it, just as Jupiter had four!

The other discovery, however, was even more important to him as a weapon against the Aristotelians. He found that the planet Venus went through phases like the moon. In the different times of the planet's course through the sky, it appeared as a new moon, a quarter-moon, a half-moon, and then a full moon. Carefully he copied his observations into his notebook.

One of the best Aristotelian arguments against Copernicus concerned Venus, the brightest planet in the sky, called by many the "evening star." If, as the astronomers believed, Venus shone with her own light and not the reflected light of the sun then Venus had to be moving about the earth and not about the sun. For if both Venus and the earth circled the sun, there would be times when Venus would appear four times brighter than ever observed.

The discovery that Venus did indeed reflect the light of the sun fulfilled the predictions of the Copernican system of the universe. Galileo was able to show that at the times when astronomers had predicted that Venus would be four times brighter, the planet was only partially reflecting the sun's light.

It did not take Galileo long to renew old acquaintances and to make new friends in Florence. He met Filippo Salviati, a Tuscan nobleman eighteen years younger than himself. Though banking was his business, Filippo had a deep interest in science, and soon he was one of Galileo's most faithful followers and defenders. Salviati had a beautiful villa high in the hills on the outskirts of Florence, and there Galileo went often to enjoy hours of discussion and entertainment.

Another man who became a loyal disciple of Galileo was Father Benedetto Castelli, a poor but learned monk from Montecassino who had come to the University of Pisa as professor of mathematics. Castelli had become convinced that the new astronomy was the true one. Like Galileo, he disagreed entirely with the claim that nothing was new in the heavens other than that which men saw with their naked eyes.

One afternoon, Galileo sat with Salviati on a stone terrace of the latter's villa overlooking the beautiful valley of the Arno River. They had been discussing the significant discovery of the phases of Venus.

"How beautifully everything falls into a pattern, Filippo! It is like watching the pieces of a puzzle come together in exactly the right way. With the sun as the center of the world, all these unexplained things are easily understood. For example, take the problem of the changing brightness of the planets. For hundreds of years now, it has been obvious to astronomers that the planets we see from the earth do not always have the same brightness. Sometimes Mars is very bright, and sometimes its light can hardly be seen. In the same way, Venus changes from bright to dim. If, as the Aristotelians would have it, each of these planets moves about the earth, then their brightness should always be the same. Of course, in order to get around this problem, astronomers resorted to imagining that the planets spun in little circles while moving in their circular paths. Then the orbit of the planet looks like this—" Galileo bent and traced a series of loops on the flagstones with his forefingers.

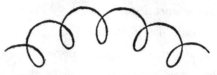

"But this, Filippo, has only led to a very complicated geometrical method of predicting the motions of the planets, without really answering the question."

"Ah, I begin to understand!" cried Salviati. "If the planets move about the sun, and the earth is just another planet doing the same thing—why, then, there must be times when the earth is nearer to Venus and times when the two are far apart."

"Bravo! That is the exact explanation! And since the planets only reflect the sun's light, their brightness does not vary as much as you would expect if they had their own light. One doesn't have to invent crazy kinds of motions to understand what is happening."

"I never really understood that before! When one reads Latin textbooks on astronomy, the language makes the ideas too complex to understand."

"Filippo, you have touched upon a sore spot! These Aristotelian professors have succeeded in making knowledge a kind of mysterious, hidden thing which only members of their own guild can understand. But why shouldn't other intelligent men besides university professors learn about new discoveries and ideas in science? After all, the world is governed by kings and princes; wars are fought by generals;

markets are controlled by merchants and bankers—these are the men who lead the world!"

"Being a banker myself, I can hardly disagree with you."

"And yet, look at the conspiracy—yes, that's what it is, a conspiracy—in the academic world to keep men from understanding any new knowledge! Well, I have decided that as far as I am concerned, from now on my articles and books are going to be written for all intelligent men, not just university people. Filippo, everything I publish will be written in Italian, the common language of our people, and not in Latin!"

"But that is a daring thing to do, Galileo. To write about scholarly matters in the common tongue will only infuriate the university authorities further."

"Frankly, I have decided that my real enemies *are* the university professors! They follow Aristotle so blindly that they cannot even believe they own eyes. Well, if they will not accept my new ideas, perhaps the leaders in the world outside the university will. I tell you, Filippo, there is a new era of science arising. It is the science of mathematics applied to nature. No matter how much they howl, the followers of Aristotle will never be able to prevent this new science from changing the thinking of men about nature! I am as sure of this as I am that the planets move in circles about the sun."

"And count on me to be on your side when you give battle, Galileo!" Salviati moved to Galileo's side and clasped his hand firmly. "Your friends in Florence believe in you as much as do your friends in Venice."

"Look here, Filippo." Galileo regarded his friend earnestly. "You are more at home in the world of politics than I am. Don't you think my struggle against the Aristotelian professors would be helped if I could get the authorities at Rome to side with me?"

"Rome?" Salviati looked doubtful. "I don't know, Galileo. Some of the men who are close to the Pope do not look upon you with much favor. Still, if you could show them the direct evidence—"

"Yes, yes, that's exactly what I had in mind! What if I took my best telescope to Rome? Surely, those men are wise enough to believe the evidence they see with their own eyes!"

"Perhaps you are right. Yes, going to Rome might be a good idea. I am sure that the Grand Duke would make the best arrangements for your convenience. Surely, if the Pope and his followers approve of your discoveries, what can the academic Aristotelians say?"

Galileo wasted little time. He petitioned his ruler, Cosimo de Medici, for the privilege of visiting Rome as an ambassador of good will from Florence. Not only was permission granted, but Galileo was given a special coach with four beautiful horses from the Grand Duke's own stables. It was arranged that he would stay at the palace of the Tuscan ambassador in Rome.

In the spring of 1611, Galileo left for the great capital of the Papal State. By his side, on the seat, was his largest telescope, packed carefully in thick, soft cloths to protect the lenses.

His entry into Rome was a minor triumph. The Tuscan ambassador had made his visit known to the public, and a large crowd was on hand to greet Galileo when he arrived. As in Venice and Florence, the telescope that Galileo carried was the focus of attention. Everyone ooh'd and ah'd, and all fingers pointed toward it. This was the magic tube that showed the wonders in the sky!

Inside the ambassador's palace, Galileo was shown to his rooms, a luxurious suite usually reserved for persons of the highest rank. He was tired. Bouncing up and down in the carriage day after day had made his bones ache. He asked to be excused and went to bed at once. But he could not sleep. In his mind, he kept going over and over what he would say to the Roman authorities to make them understand the meaning of scientific truth.

That evening, a sumptuous banquet was prepared in honor of the famous guest from Florence. Many cardinals, men who ranked next to the Pope in power, had been invited, as well as nobleman and wealthy citizens. In all, eighty people sat at the long table in the banquet hall, eating food from golden platters and drinking from silver goblets. When Galileo was introduced, they all honored him by standing and bowing to him.

After the meal, Galileo was surrounded by the guests, who begged him to tell of his discoveries. He spoke to them of how the telescope showed plainly that the sun had to be considered the center of the world.

"But this business of the earth turning," said one cardinal, "seems very odd to me." He was a plump little man, and he waved his stubby fingers, encrusted with jeweled rings, at Galileo. "Certainly, if, as the Bible states, God made the earth for man to live upon, then God meant the earth to be the most important body in the universe. Why should the earth have to turn, if all the other bodies, which were obviously not as important to God when he made them, move around the earth?"

Galileo was about to answer the cardinal sarcastically when a calm voice near him said. "Come now, Guibaldo, it seems to me that you are involving Professor Galilei in an argument that no longer concerns mathematical reasoning. I am sure he has little time for theological problems. His mathematical problems are far more important."

The speaker was another cardinal, a tall, handsome man with clear blue eyes. He wore his beard in the fashion of the hour, trimmed short and square, with a slightly downward-curling mustache over full red lip. He smiled at Galileo in a friendly manner and asked a scientific question that changed the direction of the conversation. I must remember this man, Galileo thought; perhaps he will help me in my venture here.

Much later, when the guests had taken their leave, Giuliamo de Medici, the Tuscan ambassador, introduced Galileo to a young man of regal appearance who had stayed behind. "This is Prince Frederico Cesi, Master Galileo. He asked particularly to meet you personally."

"I have waited anxiously for this moment. Professor Galilei," said the Prince, extending his hand.

"The pleasure is mine. Your Highness," answered Galileo with the respect accorded to persons of rank. "I am looking forward to making new friends in Rome."

"Be assured of one thing, sir—you already have many friends in Rome. Your book, *A Message from the Stars*, has won allies for you throughout the city. In fact, this is why

I stayed a moment—to bring you a message from those friends."

"I am very flattered indeed."

The Prince looked questioningly at the Tuscan ambassador, who coughed politely and remarked that it was time for him to go to bed. Galileo and Prince Cesi were left alone.

"I have founded in Rome a group of men who are dedicated to the new learning that has arisen. Most of them are young noblemen, and each is interested in some particular area of science. For example, I am making a study of botanical specimens brought back from the New World. Most important, however, we have united to fight against the tired and worn ideas of the Aristotelians. We call ourselves the Academy of the Lynxes."

"That is an odd name. What inspired it?"

"The Greek myth about Lynceus, the Argonaut. He was famous for his keen eyesight. We want to see farther and more clearly than most scholars are able to see now."

"It makes me happy to know that there are such men in the world. I know only a few—Johannes Kepler, the German astronomer, and Brother Paolo Sarpi in Venice. There are so few who dare to see ahead! Most of the company who laughingly call themselves scholars live like turtles, with their heads drawn safely into their hard shells of authority."

"What I am asking. Professor, is that you join our academy. We all look to you as a leader of scientific thought. I know that we are very young, and perhaps some of the things we do or say are foolish. But if you would consent to be one of us and to lead us, it would make us very proud and happy."

Galileo could not keep from embracing Cesi. "My dear boy, you overwhelm me! You don't know, you simply don't know how wonderful it is to find men with vision who can see the brilliance of the future and not the dimness of the past. Yes, yes! Of course I shall join your academy. And together we shall show the Aristotelians that the claws of the lynx can be sharp and dangerous!"

"Excellent! This is a joyous moment for the Lynceans! But see, I am keeping you up late, and I know you have an audience with His Holiness tomorrow. I shall take my leave now, so that you can rest. Giuliamo has kindly allowed me to accompany you to the Vatican tomorrow, so I shall see you then."

Galileo put his hand out. "One moment before you go. Can you tell me the name of the man who helped me when that fat cardinal was trying to bait me into a theological trap?"

"That was Cardinal Maffeo Barberini. He is a brilliant scholar who often comes to our academy meetings. He has much influence in the Vatican. As a friend, he can be very useful to you. As an enemy, he would be very dangerous."

"Then I hope he will be my friend. I must not forget to thank him when I see him again."

Prince Cesi shook Galileo's hand warmly and left. Galileo went to bed in a happy state of mind. Cesi's words had filled him with a warm glow that eased the aching of his joints and helped him fall asleep quickly.

On the following day, they drove to the Vatican, the great palace where the Pope lived. Cesi sat in the carriage by Galileo's side, pointing out the sights of the city. Rome was a curious mixture of modern and ancient buildings. The stone arches of the great Roman Colosseum, the huge arena where ancient Romans once came in throngs to watch chariot races and gladiators fighting wild beasts, still stood at one end of the city. Near it were the stately marble columns of what had been the thriving center of ancient Rome, the Forum. The traffic was appalling—coaches and horsemen dashed through the wide avenues without heed for the many people on foot. Here and there, Galileo could see groups of Christian pilgrims come to worship in the Holy City of their faith.

The Vatican was a great marble and stone building standing next to the famous Church of Saint Peter. Even as their carriage entered the wide square before Saint Peter's, Galileo could see the dome of the church high over their heads.

"Can you believe," asked Cesi, "that this tremendous dome was completed in only two years? Pope Sixtus the Fifth poured all his energy and time into the building of it. The architect felt it would take ten years to do the job properly. But the Pope could not wait that long. Poor man, he was right, for he died in 1590, just after the dome was completed."

"This church is a magnificent piece of architecture." Galileo turned to Giuliamo and asked if they had a little time to look around. The ambassador thought they might be able to spare about fifteen minutes. Galileo descended from the carriage and gazed at the church. The entrance was flanked by eight magnificent marble columns. He saw that the east wing was still under construction.

"Let's take a look at what the workmen are doing." Galileo beckoned Cesi to accompany him.

The ground was littered with piles of timber, great pieces of stone, and sheets of lead. Here and there were vast cubic stacks of bricks. Workmen moved rapidly to and fro, dragging huge timbers with long ropes to the walls, mixing batches of mortar in giant tanks, and carrying bricks in wooden hods to the bricklayers.

"Notice that the outer walls are resting on new wooden piles sunk into the ground. On this side of the church stood the circus of Nero. The original east wall had been built on its ruins. But six years ago the church began to lean over on this side. One day a great stone fell from the roof. It was a miracle that none of the congregation was killed. Pope Paul the Fifth had the whole eastern section torn down."

Galileo nodded seriously. "God moves in strange ways. Here is this magnificent Church of Saint Peter built on the very ground where the Emperor Nero had the Christians thrown to the lions!"

They walked slowly along the east wall, observing the construction work. Suddenly Galileo pointed. "Look! Those workmen over there! Aren't they mixing cement in a—a— yes, in a marble tub?"

Cesi laughed. "That's right! It is a marble tub, and a very famous one, too! That is the marble tomb of Pope Urban the Sixth. You see, in 1588, the work on the dome proceeded with tremendous haste. Orders had been given that nothing was to stand in the way. One day the workmen needed one more tank in which to mix mortar, but none could be found. So, the architect ordered the marble coffin to be used for the mixing. One day, the bones of the good Pope will be re-placed. Meanwhile, his tomb is still being used to help build this wonderful church."

Galileo laughed along with Cesi. "Oh, what a wonderful story! I must remember to tell it to my friends in Florence when I return."

It was time for the audience with Pope Paul the Fifth. When Galileo entered the Papal Chamber, he witnessed a display of pomp and ceremony that was even greater than that which he had seen in the palace of the Venetian Doge. The Pope sat in state in a great room whose walls were covered with beautiful mural paintings.

His Holiness, Pope Paul the Fifth, was already an old man. He was dressed in a long white robe, but his cape, hat, and shoes were red. On the finger of one hand was the golden ring worn by each Pope, the famous Ring of the Fisherman, on which was engraved a picture of Saint Peter fishing from a boat.

Galileo knelt before the Pope and kissed the ring held out to him. This was an act of respect and reverence which every visitor to the Vatican paid to the religious leader. Then the Pope himself demonstrated his respect and admiration for Galileo's stature as a famous scientist by raising up Galileo with his own hands and conducting him to a chair next to the papal throne.

After a few minutes of polite conversation, a very old priest joined the Pope and Galileo. When he introduced himself, Galileo leaped to his feet and shook his hand warmly.

"Father Clavius! At last I have the great honor of meeting you!" He turned to the Pope. "I cannot tell Your Holiness how much this means to me. The encouragement of Father Clavius when I was a young man did much to bolster my determination to become a good mathematician."

Father Clavius smiled. "I still remember that excellent little essay you wrote on the center of gravity of bodies."

"Ah, that. It was many years ago, and I was still very young."

"Well, Father Clavius," interrupted the Pope, "what do you think of these miracles in the sky Master Galileo has written about?"

"I am an old man, Your Holiness, and have seen and heard many things. But with all apologies to Master Galileo, I must confess that I entertain some doubts about the moon's surface looking like the earth's. And the planets that revolve about Jupiter—is he certain that the telescope itself did not put them there?"

The Pope laughed. "What do you say to that, Master Galileo?"

"All I can do is to beg Your Holiness and Father Clavius to see these wonders with your own eyes. I have brought my best telescope with me. If it pleases Your Holiness, I shall set up the instrument here in the Vatican tonight, so that the spectacle of the heavens shall become visible to Your Holiness."

"You have our permission to do so. We are most curious to see these strange sights."

The Pope waved his hand to indicate that the interview was over. With another motion, he indicated that Galileo could go, but that Father Clavius was to remain.

When Galileo described the audience to Prince Cesi, the latter nodded approvingly. "A most favorable sign. His Holiness is a very reserved man and very solemn, and such a pleasant attitude is very unusual for him."

That night, Galileo set his telescope up in the great chamber of the Pope in the Vatican. He pointed the lens at Jupiter, visible through the open window as a faint star. A chair was arranged so that His Holiness could sit comfortably while he observed the sky. Galileo focused the telescope on the planet and asked the Pope to peer into the tube.

"Why—why—!" The Pope became as excited as all the others who had ever looked through Galileo's instrument. "Is that little ball Jupiter? There are three little stars on one side of it."

"The Medicean Planets, Your Holiness."

"Come, Clavius, you must see this! Unbelievable, simply unbelievable!"

Father Clavius took his place at the eyepiece. When he looked away, there was an expression of utter bewilderment on his face. Next, Galileo showed them the countless stars of the Milky Way. As a finale, when the moon had risen, the Pope and Father Clavius were able to see the craters and the mountains.

"Master Galileo," cried the Pope, "this is a great miracle indeed!"

"I am gratified, Your Holiness." replied Galileo. "If Your Holiness will allow it," he added, "I shall be happy to send Your Holiness a telescope upon my return to Florence."

The Pope beamed. "It would make us most happy to receive one of your wonderful telescopes."

Galileo looked at Father Clavius. The opinion of the old mathematician meant very much to him. Father Clavius smiled and extended his hand to Galileo.

"My son, I must humbly beg your pardon for my remarks during the audience this morning. They were bad-mannered and uncalled-for. I hope you can forgive a foolish old man. As for the miracles you describe in your book, they certainly are there in the sky. A new era in scientific discovery has been opened by your telescope!"

His words gave Galileo a warm feeling. He felt that the expedition to Rome had been a master stroke. Now the religious leaders would be on his side in his war against the Aristotelian professors. He went back to Florence eager to resume his work. Galileo was determined to uncover all the evidence for the superiority of the Copernican system of the universe.

He now turned his attention to the sun itself. He realized at once that it would be impossible to look at the sun's surface through the telescope without blinding himself. After a few days of experimenting, he learned how to smoke the lens to make it dark enough for the sun to appear as a yellowish disk. Then he began to observe the sun every clear day.

One afternoon, as Galileo watched the sun, he saw what appeared to be flecks of dirt on its surface. With some irritation he supposed that dust had fallen on the lens. He cleaned the glass carefully and browned the lens again with smoke. But when he looked again, the spots were still there on the left side of the disk.

Could it possibly be, he asked himself, that the sun has imperfections too? If such a thing were true, then this discovery would put an end forever to the Aristotelian superstition about the perfection of heavenly bodies. The following day, the spots were still there. But something about them was different. They had moved to the right a bit!

Galileo watched carefully for the next four days. Fortunately, the weather was clear, and there were few clouds to hide the sun. He had not been mistaken. The spots were not only part of the sun, but they were moving slowly across the sun's surface! What did this mean?

There was only one answer, he decided. Not only was the sun an imperfect body, but it rotated on its axis! If the sun turned, why could not the earth turn to cause day and night on its voyage about the sun? He could not bear to leave the telescope, even though his eyes burned from the sun's brilliance. But he took the time to drop a note to Father Castelli at Pisa to tell him of the discovery of the sunspots.

> *This is the end of all claims that the Aristotelian system is the true picture of the world. Copernicus is established as the king of astronomers! The sun is not only the center of the world, but it turns on its axis! Think of it, Castelli, what a marvelous scene! The shining star we call the sun out there in space. All about it whirl the other planets in great circles, while one moon circles the earth and four moons circle Jupiter. And Saturn has two satellites which move about it. In the center of it all, the noble sun rotates slowly! And far, far out in space, the innumerable stars of the universe shine in their places in the sky. It is overwhelming! Now we can see how marvelous are the works of God!*

During the next few years, Galileo published letters and pamphlets about his observations. He wrote a series called Letters on the Solar Spots in which he tried to show that the Copernican astronomy was true.

Meanwhile, a new kind of trouble came to plague him. Unscrupulous men, trying to gain personal recognition and fame, began to write books in which they claimed authorship of Galileo's inventions and discoveries. This was not the first time. In 1607, a teacher at Padua named Capra had written a book in which he claimed that he had invented the Geometrical and Military Compass. Galileo did not have much trouble getting witnesses to attest in court to his invention of the instrument long before Capra claimed to have invented it. The university authorities had punished Capra—and Galileo had made another enemy.

Now a German priest named Father Scheiner published a letter in which he claimed to have discovered the spots on the sun before Galileo. Scheiner wrote that the spots were really many little planets like the moons of Jupiter moving about the sun. In his answer, Galileo showed easily that he had written about the solar spots long before Father Scheiner had seen them. The spots could not be little planets. Galileo had observed that often they had spread out and disappeared like clouds as they moved across the sun's surface. So, Father Scheiner became another of those who hated Galileo.

At the same time that Galileo became concerned with these scientists who were trying to rob him of his fame, another danger appeared. Monks began to preach in public against the Copernican system of the universe. They insisted that to teach that the sun was the center of the universe was heresy.

Galileo was aware of what was going on. He knew that these monks were in league with the Aristotelian astronomers against him. But he was not afraid. His success at Rome had made him bold. Let those foolish monks try to confuse people by mixing religion and science, he thought. The Pope and his cardinals surely understand that I have no heresy in mind. And their opinion is far more important than what these rabble-rousing preachers think!

He wrote a booklet about the ideas of Archimedes on the laws of bodies floating in water. In this he utterly demolished the Aristotelian argument that ice was heavier than water and floated only because of its peculiar shape. The name of the booklet was *A Discourse on Floating Bodies*, and it became a sensation in Florence overnight.

Strangely enough, he had been led to the writing of the *Discourse* by an argument at the court of the Grand Duke with some of the Aristotelian professors from the University of Pisa. By a coincidence, Cardinal Maffeo Barberini was visiting Cosimo de Medici at the same time. The cardinal took part in the discussion and appeared to enjoy the way in which Galileo made the other learned doctors look foolish. After the battle, he congratulated Galileo warmly.

"I am pleased that Your Eminence favors my point of view," said Galileo. "I still remember with gratitude how you helped me avoid an unpleasant scene in the Vatican a year ago."

"Men who are truly intellectual must stand together." Cardinal Barberini put a comradely hand on Galileo's shoulder. "It was my greatest pleasure to participate in a scientific discussion as an ally of the great Galileo. I look forward to your next visit to Rome."

Upon hearing these words of praise from a man of such high position in the Vatican, Galileo felt quite secure in his battle for scientific truth. *A Discourse on Floating Bodies* sold many copies. To Galileo's immense satisfaction, many noblemen in Florence began to study mathematics after reading the booklet.

Nevertheless, his enemies did not remain quiet for long. Galileo discovered that they were trying to spread lying accusations against him at the Grand Duke's court. He found this out only when a letter from Father Castelli in Pisa reached him in March of 1613.

I must report an incident which disturbed me greatly. At a court dinner here last week, I was challenged by the Grand Duchess Cristina. Her Highness was very concerned about the teaching of Copernican astronomy. She had been told by some of the good doctors in Florence that such teaching was against what was written in the Bible. I tried to defend it as best I could. But this is a matter which needs the attention of the Master himself. I believe that this is a deliberate attempt by your enemies to arouse the religious authorities against you. It is serious enough to demand your immediate attention.

Galileo was annoyed. He had not realized the Aristotelian professors would go so far. This was a matter that called for careful and thorough action. Choosing his words deliberately, he wrote a letter to the Grand Duchess Cristina. In it, he tried to make her understand the difference between the *religious* truths in Holy Scripture and the *scientific* truths that were to be found in nature itself. Religious truths were a matter of faith in God which he, Galileo, certainly had. But scientific truths were a matter of mathematics and reason. The men who had written the Bible were holy men; but they were not scientists. The proper attitude was to understand that the discovery of scientific truths served only to make the wonders of God more wonderful than ever.

Galileo made a copy of this letter and sent it to Father Castelli, who was overjoyed. Here was an explanation by the Master which showed clearly that there was no heresy involved in the new astronomy. He showed the letter to some of the Aristotelian astronomers at the university in order to convince them.

This was a mistake. The professors realized that what Galileo had written to the Grand Duchess could be twisted to sound as though he opposed Holy Scripture. The Aristotelians and the monks who had begun to preach against Copernicus denounced Galileo in public for criticizing the Bible. In their sermons, the monks called all mathematicians "henchmen of the Devil!" One man went so far as to demand that Copernicus be thrown in jail by the Inquisition, even though that great astronomer had been dead for seventy years.

The hullabaloo raised against Galileo had its effect. In Rome, the authorities became alarmed, and the machinery of the Inquisition was set in motion. The Holy Office moved slowly and quietly, but its methods were very thorough. Two years passed before Galileo became sufficiently aware of the danger to be worried.

He wrote letters to Prince Cesi and to Cardinal Barberini, asking them to stand by him. He sent a copy of the letter to the Grand Duchess Cristina to Cardinal Bellarmine, head of the Holy Office (the official title of the Inquisition in Rome), so that there would be no misinterpretation of what he had written. But Galileo was an honest man. He believed in wisdom and goodness and truth. To ensnare him in a network of lies was as easy for his enemies as trapping an innocent kitten.

In December of the year 1615, Galileo decided to go to Rome to plead his own case, before the Inquisition should make any decisions on the basis of his enemies' lies. At the Villa Medici, he was greeted by the new Florentine ambassador to Rome, Piero Giucciardini. The ambassador seemed to be ill at ease.

"How soon can you arrange an audience with the Pope?" asked Galileo.

The ambassador threw up his hands. "Who knows? The times are difficult. His Holiness is always busy with the construction of new buildings. It is not easy to get an audience now."

"But all you have to do is tell them that Professor Galilei is here. Surely, that should be enough!"

Giucciardini looked at him oddly. "I tell you, Master Galileo, it is a difficult matter. Perhaps it would have been better if you had not come. There are many rumors."

"What rumors?"

"Unhealthy ones." The ambassador shrugged. "For some reason, the Holy Office is displeased with you. In all truth, I must tell you, sir, that my embassy has lost favor with His Holiness because of this trouble."

Galileo saw that the ambassador resented his presence. Well, he thought, let Giucciardini be afraid for his own neck. This matter means more to the world than his petty diplomacy.

"Never mind," he said curtly, "I shall seek an audience through my personal friends. Rest assured, Signor Giucciardini, I will involve you as little as possible."

The ambassador smiled sourly. "I am afraid that if you are involved with the Holy Office, then Tuscany is involved. If Tuscany is involved, then I am involved. Good night, Master Galileo."

A surly wretch, said Galileo to himself as he prepared for bed. I can see that I can expect no help from him.

In the morning he began the work of locating his friends. Prince Cesi pledged himself to do all he could to help Galileo, as did the other members of the Academy of Lynxes. Cardinal Barberini could not be reached. Galileo found that, apart from a few loyal friends, Rome seemed to have forgotten about him and the telescope. He was no longer the greatest of all scientists, to whom the people came in awe and respect. He was just another luckless fellow in trouble with the Inquisition. People wanted to have as little to do with him as possible.

Two months dragged by. It was the middle of February. Galileo had been unable to see the Pope or any other high official in the Vatican, despite the continued attempts of Cesi and the others. Even a letter from the Grand Duke Cosimo himself had produced no effect.

The weather in Rome was raw and damp. Galileo was sick for days at a time. He spent his fifty-second birthday in bed. His bones ached and he had a fever. But he would not give up the struggle for truth.

Finally the summons came. A messenger brought a letter which ordered him to be in Cardinal Bellarmine's chambers the following morning. The word "ordered" bothered Galileo a little. But he was too relieved to care. Now he would have a chance to plead his case so that these men would really understand that he was not a heretic.

Cardinal Roberto Bellarmine was an old, heavy-set man with a serious face. He looked as though all the troubles of the world were resting on his shoulders. When Galileo entered the chamber, he saw Bellarmine sitting there in his red cardinal's cape and hat, examining a sheaf of official documents. A few other men were in the room, but Galileo paid little attention to them.

The cardinal turned and looked fully at Galileo, The scientist, gazing back at the wrinkled, brooding face of the theologian, was filled with a sense of foreboding. There was a brief silence.

"Your Eminence," Galileo burst out, "I am grateful for this opportunity to defend myself against these slanders which have been raised against me!"

He was about to continue when Bellarmine raised his hand for silence. "Master Galileo, there is no need for you to say anything. The Holy Office has already reached a decision in your case."

"A decision? But I have not yet—"

"You are in no position to question the action of the Holy Office, Master Galileo. I will read the decision to you." He sorted out one of the papers and held it up to the light. Galileo was dumbfounded at this turn of events.

"It has been decided by the General Congregation of the Inquisition that the following statements are contrary to Holy Scripture and therefore dangerous:

"*One:* That the sun is the center of the world and does not move.

"*Two:* That the earth is not the center of the world and immovable; it moves about the sun and also rotates on its own axis.

"Wherefore Master Galileo Galilei, Professor of Mathematics at Florence, is ordered to abstain from lecturing upon or teaching this opinion. If he does not do so, steps will be taken to imprison him."

Galileo was aghast. He had not expected this at all. He stood before Bellarmine, trembling with anger and indignation.

"What say you, Master Galileo?" asked Bellarmine. His voice was low and calm, yet it held a warning. "Will you swear to follow the dictates of your Church and abstain from teaching these ideas? Will you sign this pledge?"

"But—but—" faltered Galileo—" if I could only have an opportunity to show Your Eminence that the Copernican astronomy is not—"

"That is no longer possible. The writings of Copernicus on astronomy have been banned from further publication until certain corrections have been made in them. Will you sign?"

Many thoughts flashed through Galileo's mind in a short moment. He thought of his father and the search for truth. If he refused to sign, he might rot in prison for the rest of his life. It might even be worse—he remembered that the monk Giordano Bruno had been burned at the stake for his beliefs. He could hear Brother Sarpi saying, "—they are afraid of any kind of change!"

And there was so much left for him to finish—the experiments, the observations, the books . . .

Dumbly, Galileo reached for the pen and scratched his name across the bottom of the sheet. He was a faithful member of his Church. He could not go against the dictates of his own religious leaders, even if they were wrong. Perhaps there would be a chance to discuss the matter later, to show them that science—

"You have made a wise decision." Bellarmine's voice brought him back to the reality of the moment. "Believe me, Master Galileo, His Holiness thinks of you with deep respect. He understands how easy it is for a man who is always seeking new knowledge to stray from the wisdom of our Fathers. His Holiness is a very forgiving man."

The other men signed their names to the document as witnesses, and the interview was over. Galileo walked from the cardinal's chambers in a daze. He still could not believe what had happened.

Is this the end, he asked himself; is this all? Can the work of a lifetime disappear so quickly because of a few frightened men?

Suddenly the shock of the interview wore off, and Galileo was filled with deep disgust. How blind he had been! How easily his enemies had defeated him! But he had learned a lesson. He was not going to give up so easily. He would learn to be as crafty as they. Galileo clenched his fists and stared up at the sky.

Even the Inquisition cannot stop the earth from moving about the sun, he thought. This is the way God made the heavens. They can make me sign papers until they are blue in the face, he said to himself. The laws of nature will never change!

Chapter XI

Galileo returned from Rome a dejected and bitter man. He wanted only to get away from people. He sold his house and bought an estate in the hills, on the outskirts of Florence. Here/high above the Arno River valley, there was peace and quiet. He pruned his olive trees and experimented with grafting different kinds of grapevines.

Working with his hands relaxed him. He began to think about science again. Old comrades and new disciples came to his door, and he could not turn them away. Soon the Galileo of old was back, sitting in his garden, playing the lute and singing for his eager pupils. Often they talked far into the night about books, painting, music, and science.

Nevertheless, he decided that it was time to begin his scientific work again. He was afraid to write anything about Copernican astronomy, however. Every move that he made, every word that he uttered was being noted by the Inquisition. It was difficult for him to settle down to creative work. But there were some calculations to be made which he had put aside some time ago concerning the positions of the moons of Jupiter. The mathematics was laborious and difficult, but it made him forget his previous troubles. He even began to work out a method for using the moons of Jupiter to find the longitude of a ship at sea.

He missed most the old friends who would never visit him again. Filippo Salviati had died suddenly while Galileo was in Rome. Soon after, the news came of Pinelli's death. But one of the worst blows came in 1620, when the sad news came from Venice that Sagredo had passed away. As if this were not enough, the Grand Duke of Florence, Cosimo de Medici, died that same year. Now Galileo had lost his princely protector. The Grand Duchess Cristina was in power until her son Ferdinand would be old enough to rule. But Galileo remembered that she had once been swayed against him by his enemies. He could not depend upon her to protect him.

In 1623, however, an event occurred in Rome which gave Galileo new hope. Cardinal Maffeo Barberini, the man who had defended and praised Galileo publicly, was elected Pope and took the name of Pope Urban the Eighth.

"You have nothing to fear from His Holiness," wrote Prince Cesi in a joyful letter from Rome. "When I entered the Vatican, his first words were of you. He wants you to come to Rome and visit him. He pleads for you to write some new scientific papers and to send them to him. I feel that the winds at Rome have changed. The storm is over. It will be safe to sail on the ship of Copernicus."

In his excitement at the news, Galileo forgot his aching bones and the chills and flushes of fever. He had been wanting to expose an Aristotelian astronomer named Father Grassi, who had published a pamphlet attacking Copernican astronomy, calling it contrary to the Bible. Galileo worked day and night, finished the manuscript in October, and dedicated it to Pope Urban. The Vatican quickly granted approval for its publication, and Cesi arranged for the printing and distribution under the auspices of the Academy of Lynxes. The pamphlet, which Galileo entitled *Il Saggiatore,* meaning "The Assayer," was an immediate success. In it, Father Grassi's ideas were picked apart with scathing wit and flung to the winds.

Galileo waited until the spring of 1624 before setting out for Rome. Long-distance riding during the winter was far too difficult for him. But as the sun's rays grew warmer, and green buds began to swell on tree branches, he prepared for his trip.

He arrived first at Prince Cesi's summer villa in the town of Acquasparte, where he spent a few weeks soaking up the warm sunshine.

"Pope Urban cannot wait for your arrival," Cesi assured him. "He keeps asking over and over, 'When is Galileo coming?' He is extremely flattered by your dedication. Oh, you will find things different in Rome from what they were eight years ago."

Cesi was right. Things were different in Rome. Now that the Pope had publicly approved of Galileo, the scientist was again the focus of all attention. Galileo's enemies had faded into the background. They were powerless to attack him.

On the day following his arrival in Rome, Galileo received an audience with Pope Urban the Eighth. The Pope would not allow Galileo to kneel. He embraced the scientist warmly and led him to a seat.

"How good it is to see you! We have waited too long for your visit. Your masterful answer to Grassi pleased us very much. He is utterly demolished! But tell us, on the point that you make against his statement that the ancient Babylonians cooked eggs by whirling them in slings—"

So began the first of a series of weekly discussions between Galileo and the Pope. His Holiness received Galileo with such open delight on that first day, that the scientist left the audience in a kind of happy daze. As he turned a corner in the corridor, a thump that almost knocked him down brought him back to reality. He had bumped into a fat priest so huge that his robe would have covered two ordinary men.

Galileo's eyes widened as he recognized the man. "Nicky? It isn't little Nicky Riccardi of Florence? What are you doing here?"

The priest grasped Galileo's hand and shook it warmly. His loosely girdled belly shook with pleased laughter.

"Galileo! The Wrangler himself! I have been waiting to meet you. Cesi told me you were coming."

"But you—a priest in the Vatican?"

"You are now looking at the Master of the Holy Palace. And at not such a little Nicky, I'm afraid. Why, it was I who put the seal of approval on the publication of your answer to Grassi. That's my job—to license all books for publishing."

"Congratulations! That's a very responsible position. And what did you think of my answer to Grassi?"

"Who in Florence does not recognize the wit of Master Galileo? A masterpiece! Grassi is shrunken to a nothing! But, frankly, I don't know what all the shouting is about. Why grown men want to waste valuable time arguing about how the heavens move is beyond me!"

"Why is it a waste of time?" asked Galileo.

Father Riccardi shrugged his massive shoulders. "Because there is one simple explanation that solves everything. Every star and every planet in the sky is moved by its own particular angel. That's all there is to it, and it's none of our business!"

Galileo laughed good-naturedly. "Stick to your beliefs, Niccolo! In the long run, you are the one who will have no problems. But, seriously, you must come and visit me at Prince Cesi's palace, and we'll talk over old times."

"I will, be assured." Father Riccardi bent toward Galileo and spoke in a confidential tone. "And I think I can tell you that the trouble of the past can be forgotten. His Holiness thinks poorly of those who slandered your name. But his opinion of you is of the highest."

Galileo thanked his old friend and repeated his cordial invitation. He was now more hopeful than ever that he would be able to get the Pope to reverse the decree of 1616 against the teaching of Copernican astronomy.

But by the end of the sixth and last audience, Galileo realized that Barberini as cardinal was one man; as Pope, he was another. All hints that Galileo made about being allowed to teach Copernican astronomy freely were politely turned aside. Galileo was smothered in compliments and frustrated by small talk.

Finally he understood what Pope Urban meant. It was all very well to discuss the Copernican system as a sort of interesting after-dinner game. It was fun to make up different mathematical exercises about the motions of the stars and the planets.

But theology had to be left strictly alone! Since Copernican astronomy seemed to conflict with statements about the heavens in the Bible, such ideas could not be taught as gospel truth.

As for the edict of 1616, forbidding Galileo to teach such an astronomy, that had to stand. It was not good policy, the Pope explained, for the Holy Office to reverse its decisions. Such action only weakened its prestige and aided its enemies. But Galileo could understand that the edict of 1616 might be overlooked, as long as his scientific statements did not appear to contradict Holy Scripture.

Galileo left Rome with mixed feelings. He was sad because he had not quite succeeded in getting the Pope to see the real meaning of Copernican astronomy. Yet Galileo was happy because the Pope had implied that he was now free to write or talk about the ideas of Copernicus. The Pope had made it clear that such ideas were not heretical. For Galileo, the words of the Pope were a clear signal to go ahead. He was ready to begin writing his great book on the workings of the universe.

He planned the book carefully. There were two important things he had to do. First, all the evidence for the mathematical superiority of the Copernican system had to be fitted together to form a completely convincing picture. Secondly, the scientific explanations had to be clear and simple enough to be understood by any intelligent man. A few months after his return to Florence, he began writing the book. True to his promise to Salviati, he wrote in the Italian language instead of Latin.

The title he chose for this work was *A Dialogue on the Ebb and Flow of the Sea*. He planned to use an explanation of the ocean tides to prove that the earth moved about the sun and rotated on its own axis. The arguments were presented in the form of a conversation between three people, like a play written for the stage.

The leading character he named Salviati, after his dear friend in Florence. He pictured Salviati as a wise searcher for the truths of nature, a man who was able to explain scientific principles in a way easy to understand.

The second actor on the stage was called Sagredo, after the Venetian friend he had left so many years before. Sagredo was an intelligent and curious man, always asking questions about scientific theories, always trying to separate in his mind bad evidence from good.

The third person in the dialogue was named Simplicius, which was the Latin word for "simpleton." Galileo left no doubt as to whom Simplicius represented. He was all the foolish Aristotelian professors put together. He believed anything he read, as long as it was written by someone listed as an authority on what Aristotle said. His questions showed that he understood very little about scientific reasoning or mathematics. But Galileo used Simplicius as a means of asking simple questions—the kind most difficult to answer.

Work on the book went slowly. There were many interruptions, mostly duties he had to perform for the Grand Duchess Cristina. Armories for military weapons had to be built; the young Ferdinand needed tutoring in mathematics; the city sewerage system needed changing. Again, the bouts of pain and fever held him up for weeks at a time. The court physician came to draw blood from Galileo's veins. He dosed him with the latest medicines. But nothing helped. It was only a matter of staying in bed until the fever left him. And Michelangelo came from Germany to live off Galileo like a leech.

Gradually the book was written. The arguments in it went beautifully, so beautifully that Galileo was quite carried away. He forgot that he was supposed to be presenting the Copernican system as an exercise in mathematics. In one part, he had Salviati say, "It is true that the Copernican system upsets the Aristotelian world very much, but we are concerned with *the real and actual universe!*"

Following these words he wrote, "Copernicus has arranged the world so, because God has placed the sun in the center, where it can shine its light on all the planets and not off to one side."

In another part he made fun of the Aristotelian professors by saying, "I think we ought not to bother with those imbeciles who say that it is impossible for the earth to be rotating, because they cannot have lunch in Turkey and dinner in Japan."

This was in answer to one professor who claimed that if the earth did turn on its axis, it would be observed to turn under a person suspended in the air. Galileo showed that there was no way for any person to know that the earth was turning by performing an experiment while on the earth. It was a question of realizing that the senses could be deceived by the apparent motion of the sun.

Another argument that Galileo called idiotic was the claim that the earth was much too heavy to climb over the sun and fall back again. "No," he wrote, "what can you do with people who are too stupid to understand their own stupidity?"

It took him five long years to write the book. Now the important thing was to get his book published. Prince Cesi wrote and suggested that the wise thing to do was to bring the manuscript in person to Rome for approval.

Perhaps it would be best, thought Galileo after he had read Cesi's letter. But I am sixty-six years old now. He walked up and down the hall of his house, pausing a moment before the mirror on the wall. The face he saw was lined, and the beard was streaked with white. He had begun to lose some of his hair. Still, he said to himself, this is a journey I must make.

In May, Galileo arrived in Rome, bearing his bulky manuscript and a letter of introduction to the new Florentine ambassador, Francesco Niccolini. Niccolini proved to be far more friendly than the previous ambassador, Giucciardini. He promised to help Galileo as much as possible to get papal approval for his book.

His Holiness, Pope Urban the Eighth, seemed extremely happy to see Galileo again. They had a long talk, during which Galileo described the contents of his *Dialogue*.

"Your Holiness can see," he concluded, "that the argument is built upon harmless mathematical speculation. I propose to show how the Copernican theory simplifies the calculations of astronomy. Also, I try to make an ingenious argument to show that if a person is on the earth, he cannot determine in any way whether the earth is moving."

"This *Dialogue* of which you speak sounds stimulating and unobjectionable to us," answered the Pope. "However, we have a few suggestions to make. In the first place, the title does not please us. This business of the tides is very misleading. Why, it might sound to some as though you were using this to demonstrate that the motion of the earth is real. Why not call it a dialogue about the two astronomical systems of the universe?"

"An excellent suggestion, Your Holiness," agreed Galileo diplomatically. "The title has a majestic sound. *A Dialogue on the Two Great Systems of the World!* I shall make this change at once."

"Another thing. We think that the Preface should be a little more to the point about your treating the Copernican system as a mathematical exercise. You understand our meaning there. And the ending of the book must emphasize in no uncertain way the following argument." The Pope paused a moment in thought and then went on.

"Since God can do anything in any possible way, man cannot ever hope to prove anything about nature. You see, my dear Galileo, if you try to prove that the earth moves by using, let us say, the tides as evidence, why, then you are saying that the universe exists only in this one possible way. Now, that means that you are limiting the all-powerfulness of God. We hope you understand our argument."

Galileo did not understand the argument at all. It made no sense to him. But he knew he had to have the Pope's approval. "Rest assured, Your Holiness, the final words of my book shall repeat your very words!"

"Then we see no reason why your book should not be published. We shall take steps to inform Father Riccardi that your manuscript seems acceptable to us. Of course, he will have to check the actual manuscript himself."

Exhausted by the agony of waiting, but joyous over the outcome of his audience with Urban the Eighth, Galileo brought the *Dialogue* to Father Riccardi. The corpulent Master of the Holy Palace took the bulky manuscript and made a wry face.

"Your book is almost as wide as I am," he joked. "Well, Master Galileo, we'll soon have this official permission cleared up for you. While you're writing a new Preface and ending, as His Holiness specified, I'll have my assistant go through the manuscript and check small things. For your own protection," he added apologetically.

Galileo smiled. "I understand, Niccolo. But I hope you won't delay too long. I am anxious to have this book published as soon as possible."

"I give you my word." With this assurance, Father Riccardi bore the manuscript away to his office in the inner recesses of the Vatican.

Galileo worked hard to write a new Preface. He wrote an extra last page to the book in which he put the Pope's words about the power of God into the mouths of his characters. He brought the finished work to Father Riccardi.

The fat Master of the Holy Palace looked embarrassed. "I don't know if I can place the seal of approval on this immediately. Some of my workers have gone through the manuscript very carefully. It was for your own protection, Galileo," he added quickly, upon seeing the look of dismay on Galileo's face. "I have marked the places where they think changes should be made."

Galileo guessed that some of his enemies had been whispering in Father Riccardi's ear. "Please, Nicky, for the sake of our old friendship, give me permission to publish the book in Rome. I can't stay in the city any longer, the summer is too hot."

"Well—" Father Riccardi scratched at his bald pate. "All right, I'll grant permission. But only on condition that you return to Florence and make the necessary changes in the book."

"I plan to return to Rome and arrange for the printing as soon as the weather is cool enough." Galileo knew that little work would be accomplished during the hot and humid Roman summer.

"Good, good," sighed Father Riccardi. "I shall await your return anxiously." He handed the heavy manuscript to Galileo with a sigh that was almost relief.

Galileo rode back to Florence with the feeling that things had gone rather well. He had spoken a last word with Prince Cesi before the departure. "Do you think Riccardi will keep his word?"

"Never fear," reassured Cesi, "I will keep an eye on things here."

But Galileo had not reckoned with fate.

In July, the plague broke out with new fury in northern Italy. It was one of the most terrible visitations of the Black Death that had ever occurred. Communication between cities was almost completely cut off.

Fear gripped men's hearts. Shops were barred and shut-tered. Often the doors of houses in which plague victims lay on their beds were nailed closed, so that the sick could not get out to infect others. On the main highways, roadblocks were set up. All mails were stopped, and letters and packag-es were fumigated. Most of the time they were fumigated so well that their contents were ruined.

Galileo did not dare leave his villa to go into Florence. From his hillside, he could hear the bells in the city tolling day and night for the dead. There were no longer any regu-lar mails, and he did not know how long it might take for the Preface to be returned by Riccardi.

A letter finally came from the Tuscan ambassador. Diplomatic mail was allowed to pass through the road-blocks without fumigation. The news was all bad. Prince Cesi had died suddenly. This was a double disaster. Not only had Galileo lost a true friend, but now there was no one important enough to intercede for him at the Vatican. And to make matters worse, Galileo's enemies had some-how gotten to the Pope.

"Try to have the book printed in Florence at once," wrote Niccolini, "or you may not get it printed at all. I suggest you ask Father Riccardi to grant permission through the Inquisitor of Florence."

The cold hand of despair gripped Galileo's heart. But he shook off the fear he felt and sent a letter to Riccardi at once through the Tuscan diplomatic pouch. There was no answer from Rome.

The summer passed, and then the winter of the following year. Galileo had not yet received the Preface from Riccardi, nor had permission to publish been granted. Finally, Galileo persuaded Ferdinand, who had now become Grand Duke of Florence, to intercede for him.

"After all," pointed out the scientist, "the book is to be dedicated to Your Royal Highness. Why should there be a delay?"

Political pressure was successful. In the early autumn of 1631, the Preface was returned with the official seal of approval. The Inquisitor of Florence added his stamp of approval to the manuscript.

Galileo was quite worn out from anxiety, but he summoned all his surplus energy to work with the printer and publisher on the book. The printers worked like demons. But the book was a thick one, almost five hundred pages long. Months passed before the proofs were ready for correcting. Then the binding and covering had to be done. As Galileo sat up into the early hours of the morning correcting errors, he often felt that Vincenzio, his father, was standing behind him with a smile of approval.

In February of 1632, on his sixty-eighth birthday, Galileo arrived at the court in Florence to present the first copy of *A Dialogue on the Two Great Systems of the World* to Grand Duke Ferdinand.

As he handed the volume to the young monarch, Galileo felt that his greatest mission in life had been accomplished. He had fitted together, for all men to know, the different parts of the mysterious puzzle of nature into a whole dazzling truth.

And this truth was that man existed on a globe that spun like a top as it moved in a circle about a bright, hot, shining star.

Chapter XII

Copies of Galileo's new book sold as quickly as they were displayed in Florence bookstores. For the first time, men who were not professional scholars could read about and understand scientific ideas. When copies of the book reached Rome, Galileo's enemies realized that the *Dialogue* provided the means for his destruction. Quietly, they began to sow seeds of discord.

First, Father Riccardi was told that Galileo had made changes in the final version of the book which were contrary to the Pope's wishes. Riccardi became frightened. He jogged from one bookstore to another, trying to buy up all the copies in the city.

Meanwhile, Galileo was basking in a newly found glory. Congratulations were pouring in from everywhere. Night after night, his villa was filled with the sounds of joyous conversation and the music of his lute.

The rumor that something had gone wrong at Rome came as a surprise to Galileo. Why should there be trouble? The whole business had been accomplished in an official manner. He wrote to Florence at once to beg the Grand Duke for help. Ferdinand promised to do what he could. A message was sent to Niccolini at Rome, ordering him to go at once to the Pope to find out what was wrong.

When he entered the Pope's chamber for his audience, Niccolini saw at once that Urban the Eighth was in a poor humor. The conversation proceeded, strained and polite, until Niccolini mentioned Galileo. An astounding change took place in Pope Urban's manner. His face reddened with anger, and his eyes flashed venom. He pounded his fist on the arm of the papal throne.

"That scoundrel!" he shouted. "That ingrate! We try to befriend him. And how does he repay us? By doing all this behind our back! Well, this time he has gone too far! Let him take care! It is out of our hands now. This is a matter for the Holy Office!"

These were the words Niccolini dreaded to hear. He proceeded cautiously. "If Your Holiness could only tell me what crime Galileo has committed against the Church?"

"The Holy Office does not have to account to you or anyone else for its actions, Signor Niccolini. When it acts, the reasons are usually sufficient. But we can tell you this: Galileo has made a fool of us for the last time! We have been forgiving and patient with him. But this is too much!"

"I cannot understand how such a thing is possible! He received the official seal of approval of the Holy Office to print his book."

"Oh, yes, we know. And Father Riccardi will have some explaining to do about that! What Galileo did was pointed out to us soon enough, and we were able to see it at once! Look at the ending of his *Dialogue*. Oh, he was crafty all right! He used the words we suggested. But who speaks them? A character named Simplicius! A fool! Are our opinions to be considered only worthy of a fool's mouth?"

Niccolini tried to soothe the Pope's anger. "But I am certain, Your Holiness, that this is not what Master Galileo had in mind at all. I am sure that—"

"We do not care to discuss the matter further!" interrupted Pope Urban. "We have enough serious problems on our mind without having to worry about a mathematician's insults. As for your precious Galileo—let him take care! He has become a nuisance and a troublemaker with his Copernican astronomy and his writing about science in the Italian tongue! Scholarship belongs to the university, not to the merchant! He has gone too far!"

And with this warning, the audience was ended.

Niccolini sought out others he knew in the Vatican. All they would tell him was that Galileo was suspected of heresy. It was a very serious accusation.

As usual, the Inquisition moved slowly. Back on his farm on the hillside of Arcetri, Galileo worried. He knew something was in the wind, but had no idea of how serious matters were. Waiting and anxiety affected his health. The fever returned to sap his strength. To make matters worse, his eyesight began to fail. Years of peering through his telescopes at the sun had taken their toll.

The blow fell on the first of October. On that day, the Inquisitor of Florence appeared at Galileo's door with a summons. Galileo had thirty days in which to appear before the Holy Office at Rome. No explanation or reason was given.

Galileo hurriedly wrote to the Vatican, requesting permission to come after the winter had passed. He was afraid, he wrote, that his frail body, now almost seventy years old, would be unable to stand the rigors of such a long trip. The only answer was a harsh note refusing to permit any delay.

Grand Duke Ferdinand used his political power to keep Galileo from being taken to Rome by force. Nevertheless, the young ruler was troubled. He came to see Galileo a few months later, in January in 1633. Sitting by the scientist's bed, he urged Galileo to go to Rome.

"Once you face them openly," added Ferdinand, "your enemies will fall away. If you have done nothing wrong, you have nothing to fear. Besides, I will do all I can to protect you."

Actually, young Ferdinand was afraid of becoming involved in a war with the Papal State over Galileo. It was bad enough that there was a strong enemy, France, to the north of Tuscany. Ferdinand wished no additional trouble with his southern neighbor. And defying the Inquisition could be bad business for a ruler. The Grand Duke did not want to set himself against his church.

"You will still have the best of care," he promised Galileo. "I will send you in a comfortable litter, so that you can be resting during the entire trip. You will have the best doctors waiting attendance on you in Rome. Every comfort in the Villa Medici will be yours."

As Galileo listened to the Grand Duke, his courage returned. Why was I afraid? he thought. After all, they will not bum me at the stake! His Holiness was always my friend. The Grand Duke is right. I must go and face those scoundrels who are accusing me. I'll have no trouble defending myself against their lies.

"Yes, Your Highness," he said, "I shall go to Rome. You are right. It is better to face them."

Strangely enough, once Galileo had made the decision, he felt much better. His strength began to return. He was so confident that he would vindicate himself, that when the Venetian Senate sent a secret messenger offering Galileo sanctuary in Venice, he refused. He could not run from this battle for truth.

Galileo made the journey to Rome without difficulty and arrived on the thirteenth of February. He was tired, but filled with hope that he would triumph over his persecutors.

Ambassador Niccolini and his wife welcomed him with open arms. They lodged him in the most comfortable suite of rooms in the Villa Medici. The next morning, Niccolini requested permission from the Grand Inquisitor that Galileo be allowed to remain at the Tuscan Embassy instead of being put in prison.

"He is so weak," Niccolini told the Inquisitor, "that I am afraid imprisonment might kill him. And he has a new trouble—his eyes. Master Galileo is slowly going blind."

The favor was granted. "But, remember," warned the Inquisitor, "he must not leave your villa for any reason. Only you and Signora Niccolini may be admitted to his rooms. Failure to comply with this will result in his immediate imprisonment." Niccolini swore that this order would be faithfully obeyed.

And then—nothing. There was no word from the Holy Office for weeks. Finally, on the twelfth of April, Galileo was summoned to the Chambers of the Inquisition. However, he was not plunged into one of the dark stone dungeons in the basement. Instead, he was shown to a comfortable apartment of three rooms, with a servant to attend him. The only sign of his imprisonment was the armed guard at the door. Grand Duke Ferdinand's influence had been effective.

Now began a series of interviews, day after day, during which Galileo was badgered about Copernican astronomy. Had he not been warned about this heresy seventeen years before by Cardinal Bellarmine? Had he not sworn never to teach that the earth moved around the sun? Had he not sworn not to hold or defend such a theory? Had he received permission to write the *Dialogue?* Had he told Father Riccardi about Cardinal Bellarmine's warning in 1616?

Galileo was bewildered. He protested his innocence. He remembered nothing about being forbidden to teach Copernican astronomy. But the questions went on, over and over again. Had he not been warned? Had he not sworn? Galileo did not know what to think.

In the evenings, in his apartment, he sat and thought about what was happening. It was unreal, like a dream. A little voice deep inside him kept saying, "You are old and sick. You are going blind. They are using up the days of your life, and the work will never be finished. There is still so much work to be done!"

He shook off his feeling of depression and tried to forget the Inquisition by thinking about his next book—the volume on the new science of motion. This was the book he had planned to write years ago, in Pisa; but he had never found the time. Now he would show how neatly the laws of moving bodies were connected with the magic numbers of Pythagoras. He would include the tables of aiming angles for the use of army gunners so that they could hit their targets with precision. He would show how the pendulums had told him the truth about how bodies fell toward the earth. Thinking about the book made the time pass quickly for Galileo.

One morning, the chief interviewer, a Father Firenzuola, came to his apartment. "I will not bandy words with you, Master Galileo," he said. "Your situation is serious. No matter how you try, you cannot wriggle out. You have left yourself open to a charge of teaching and defending heretical ideas. If this investigation goes much further, who knows what will happen? The usual procedure is the torture chamber. I assume you are acquainted with what goes on in there?"

Galileo nodded with a shudder.

Firenzuola leaned forward. "Be sensible. Take the simplest way out. Admit now that you were led to perform these deeds because of—well, because of any human failing: vanity, greed, ambition. It makes no difference. Throw yourself on the mercy of the Holy Office. Then the story will be different. A serious warning, perhaps, or a light prison sentence—with the Villa Medici as your prison. Believe me, a confession would be the best way out for all of us."

Galileo sighed. In his heart, he had already decided to do the very thing Firenzuola had suggested. And now they had come to him! This was a good sign, he decided. He would soon be free to work again.

The confession was made. Signing the document was a humiliating experience for Galileo. Yet he knew it had to be done. And apparently Firenzuola had been right. The following day, Galileo was allowed to return to the Villa Medici.

"I feel a sense of shame and guilt," confessed Galileo, as he and Niccolini sat before a roaring fire in the great drawing room of the embassy.

"Guilty? You? What nonsense!"

"I should have gone to His Holiness and explained—"

"Ah, Master Galileo!" exclaimed Niccolini. "When it comes to these matters, you are a child! His Holiness is not the man you knew years before. He is sorely troubled; he has the weight of many political intrigues upon his shoulders. He is afraid of being assassinated. Your case is only another thorn in his side. If you had not signed a confession, I would have feared for your life. This business of mixing science and religion has gone beyond all reason. You did what had to be done, and no man will condemn you for it."

Galileo pulled at his beard for a moment. "Of course, you are quite right, Niccolini. I did what had to be done. Well, let's not speak of it again. It's all over."

But it was not over. Even though Galileo had signed a formal confession of guilt, there was no word from the Holy Office. Niccolini rode to the Vatican every day to find out when Galileo would be released. To his horror, he discovered that a special commission of Aristotelian professors had persuaded the Holy Office to try Galileo as a heretic. The trap had been sprung. In spite of the confession, Galileo had not escaped.

Niccolini ran to the Pope and begged His Holiness to end the trial.

Coldly, the Pope refused. "Galileo has expressed opinions which are contrary to Holy Scripture. And after he was warned not to do so! He must pay for his crimes! His book will be condemned. He may not publish books again! And he must atone personally for his sins."

"But, Your Holiness, the Grand Duke Ferdinand considers himself to be Galileo's protector!"

"It would be better if His Highness kept out of this affair which concerns only us!" The Pope waved his hand. "However, we are not without mercy. After the sentencing, perhaps we can discuss ways of lessening his punishment."

Galileo was heartsick. He knew that he would have to wait for the decision of the Inquisition. Pope Urban's words meant little. What was in store for him? Life imprisonment in a dark stone dungeon? A flaming death at the stake in a public square? He tried to shut these terrible thoughts from his mind. But the awful images haunted even his sleep.

On the twenty-first of June, Galileo was summoned to appear before the ten cardinals who were to be his judges. He came into the trial hall a bent, graying figure, walking with some difficulty. Before him, about a great semicircular table, sat the cardinals in their red cloaks and hats. Their faces were impassive. Galileo was shown to a lone chair facing the judges.

He first swore on the Bible to tell the truth about anything his judges would ask.

"Do you have any statement to make in your defense?" asked the cardinal who was to be the examiner.

"No."

"Then you will answer this question: Do you, Galileo Galilei, hold the opinion that the earth moves about the sun?"

For a moment, silence hung in the hall like an unexploded bomb. Then, in a bare whisper that sounded almost like a hoarse shout in the quiet, Galileo said, "I do not."

"Do you hold that the sun is the immovable center of the world?"

"I do not."

"Do you hold that the earth rotates on its axis as it moves?"

"I do not." Galileo felt he had to impress the judges with his sincerity. He added quickly, "I have not held these Copernican ideas since I was told that they were false. I am an old man. Do with me what you will."

"Now we must ask you again, Galileo Galilei. But this time, we warn you that if you do not tell the truth, the instruments of the torture chamber will follow." And again the same three questions were asked.

Trembling, Galileo once more denied that he believed in the earth's motion. The examiner seated himself, while the ten cardinals buzzed and nodded among themselves. Then he rang a little bell, and Galileo was escorted from the trial hall. Instead of returning to the Villa Medici, he was conducted to the apartment that had served as a prison in the quarters of the Holy Office.

"Your sentence will be read to you tomorrow," said the guard, just before he closed and locked the door.

Galileo lay on his bed in the darkness of the Inquisition building. The days of questioning and waiting were finally over. Only the agony of knowing his fate was left.

He wanted desperately to live. There was so much to be done. There were books to write, experiments to plan, mathematics to be worked out . . .

He fell into a fitful sleep full of nightmares that were half real, half dream. He seemed to hear his father's voice again, so far away that he could just make out the words.

"This is the way you must never be, my son," Vincenzio was saying. Galileo strained to hear. "Do not be afraid to challenge authority at any time, if a search for truth is in question. . . . Truth can be found only by free and open minds. . . . Do not be afraid of what others may say. . . . Seek for truth. . ."

Again Galileo started from his sleep with an exclamation. The words he had just heard in his dream echoed in his mind. What have I done? he asked himself.

He was no longer certain that he had been right to confess that his ideas were wrong. How would history remember him? Would he be the man who had fought with all his heart and soul for the truth? Or would he be despised as a traitor to science? Should he have spat defiance at the Inquisition and gone to his death like the brave Giordano Bruno?

He remembered how Sarpi had told him of Bruno's last words to the judges who had sentenced him: "You who condemn me live in greater fear than I." Would Bruno be remembered and Galileo forgotten?

The guards came for him at noon on the following day. His servant clothed him in the dress customary for prisoners of the Inquisition at their sentencing. Over his outer clothes was placed a long white shirt of rough material—the "shirt of penitence." Then slowly, for he was deathly tired, Galileo was conducted to the great hall where judgment was passed by the Holy Office on heretics and sinners.

Galileo noticed little of the hall and how his ten judges were arranged before him. Though great white candles burned brilliantly in their tall iron candlesticks all about the room, he could see the shapes of the cardinals only dimly. On the dais where they sat, their capes formed a wide red semicircle about him. At a signal from the Commissary-General, Galileo knelt before them as the sentence was read aloud.

It was a long document, and the clerk read it with a bored and droning voice. The recounting of his misdeeds against the Church seemed endless for Galileo. He began to hear the words clearly only when the reader came to the final paragraph.

"We pronounce this, our one final sentence, since you, Galileo Galilei, have been suspected by this Holy Office of a grave heresy, that is, of having held and taught opinions contrary to the Holy Scripture. You are to abandon the false opinion that the sun is the immovable center of the world and that it does not move from east to west and that the earth does move and is not the center of the world. You will be absolved of the censures and penalties that are raised against wrongdoers if you agree to renounce, curse, and hate these errors and heresies."

Why do they stretch it out so, with such a jumble of words? thought Galileo. But a faint hope crept into his heart. Would he be allowed to go free? The next sentence seemed to crush out all hope.

"But in order that your terrible error may not go altogether unpunished, and that you may be an example and a warning to others to abstain from such opinions, we decree that your book, *Dialogue on the Two Great Systems* of the World, be banned publicly; also, we condemn you to the formal prison of this Holy Office for an indefinite period convenient to our pleasure. So we, the subscribing and presiding cardinals pronounce!"

As he listened, Galileo's head dropped lower. Imprisonment! For how long? Perhaps he would rot in a stone dungeon for the rest of his life, alone and forgotten. But there was no time to think. A paper was thrust into his hand, and be was commanded to read. One of the candelabras was brought near so that he could see. A guard carried in a large Bible upon which Galileo was told to place his hand. In the gloomy silence, Galileo's voice rang hoarsely, and his speech was halting.

"I, Galileo Galilei, son of Vincenzio Galilei of Florence, aged seventy years, being brought to judgment and kneeling before you, Most Eminent Cardinals and General Inquisitors against heresy, touching the Holy Scripture with my own hands, swear that I have always believed and will in the future believe that the sun is not the center of the world and that the earth does not move.

"Since I am accused of holding and teaching this false opinion, and of writing a book in which I supported this opinion in a forceful way, I am willing to remove from the minds of Your Eminences this suspicion against me. With a sincere heart and faith, I renounce, curse, and hate these errors and heresies contrary to the Holy Scripture.

"I swear that in the future, I will nevermore write or say anything to cause such suspicions again. Moreover, if I know of any heretic who holds similar opinions, I shall denounce him to the Holy Office. If I violate any of the promises and oaths I have made, I will subject myself to all the pains and punishments decreed against me.

"I, the above named Galileo Galilei, have condemned, sworn, promised, and bound myself, and witness thereof, have signed this document with my own hand on the twenty--second of June, 1633."

As he knelt there, the pen for signing was thrust into his fingers. Galileo wrote his name, but he did not have the strength to rise. A whirlpool of sickness and shame boiled within him. He had been condemned by his own church for a crime which was not a crime in his own eyes. For revealing the truths of nature, he had been sentenced to a lifetime of prison as a liar and a heretic.

The two guards lifted him gently to his feet, and he was led to the door. Now they would chain his hands and his legs, he thought, and lead him down into the cells from which no man ever returned. Would he ever see his friends again? Would he ever sit again under a tree in his garden and play the lute? Would other men of learning ever read his as yet unwritten books?

He walked along between his guards, no longer caring, resigned to his doom. But suddenly, there was a hand on his arm, and a wonderfully familiar voice was saying, "Master Galileo! We have been waiting for you! You are free to come with us!"

It was Francesco Niccolini and his wife. Galileo did not quite believe his ears. He looked up at Niccolini with bewilderment in his eyes.

Niccolini took his hand. "It is true, Master Galileo. His Holiness has consented to release you in our custody! The Villa Medici will be your prison, but we hope you will consider it your home."

The guards had disappeared. Niccolini took Galileo's arm, and he and the Signora Niccolini walked the mathematician slowly to a waiting carriage. On the way, Niccolini muttered into Galileo's ear, "I have heard what they made you do. It is the end of science in Italy!"

Galileo waited until they were all seated in the carriage before he spoke. All at once, the same excitement that had always swelled up inside him as a boy now seethed again. The books would be written! Never mind that the Inquisition would forbid their being published. Somewhere, somehow, men would see his manuscripts, read about his ideas. The growth of science would not be stopped.

"Now I can begin my book on the new science of motion," he said to Niccolini.

"Wait a while! Let your strength return." Niccolini's face took on a puzzled look. "But your eyes, Master Galileo? Will it not be impossible for you to write—?"

"My blindness does not matter. Other hands will write for me as I dictate. My books are not in my fingers or my eyes. They are all up here." Galileo tapped his head.

Niccolini leaned back against the carriage seat and sighed. "I have heard that your sentence will be read aloud to all the mathematicians and astronomers in the universities of Italy as a warning. The teaching of Copernican astronomy is doomed."

Galileo looked out of the little window at his side. The sun was shining brightly in Rome. Here, an ancient ruined column threw a broken, twisted shadow. There, the corner of a new building formed a shadow that was sharp and angular. Galileo turned to Niccolini with a smile.

"You know, Francesco, I used to think that if this affair was ever finished, I would feel nothing but hate for all those men in the Holy Office. But it hasn't happened that way at all. I feel only pity."

"Pity? For those who condemned you?"

"After all, they tried so pitifully hard to change the laws of nature. But in spite of their condemning scientists, in spite of their imprisoning or burning us, the truths of nature are enduring. These men have blinded themselves and others to what is beautiful and true in nature—the mathematical order which governs all things.

"And above all, Francesco," Galileo added, "in spite of what they forced me to say, the earth will continue to move on its path about the sun!"

Acknowledgments

The author wishes to acknowledge his indebtedness to the following works for information about Galileo:

De Santillana, Giorgio, *The Crime of Galileo*, University of Chicago Press, Chicago, 1955.

Fahie, J. H., *Galileo*, John Murray, London, 1903.

Namer, Emile, *Galileo*, Robert McBride, New York, 1936.

Olney, Mrs., *Private Life of Galileo*, London, 1870.

The following works of Galileo have been translated into English and published in the United States:

Dialogue on the Great World Systems, Salusbury translation. University of Chicago Press, Chicago, 1953.

Dialogue Concerning the Two Chief World Systems, translated by Stillman Drake, University of California Press, Berkeley, 1953.

Dialogue Concerning Two New Sciences, translated by Crew and De Salvio, Dover Publications, New York, 1914.

ACKNOWLEDGMENTS

Discoveries and Opinions of Galileo, translated by Stillman Drake, Doubleday Anchor Books, New York, 1957 ("The Starry Messenger," "Letters on the Sunspots," "Letter to the Grand Duchess Cristina," "The Assayer").

About the Author

Sidney Rosen (1916–2005) was born in Boston and graduated with a bachelor's degree from the University of Massachusetts and a PhD from Harvard University. He gained tenure at the University of Illinois, where he taught in the astronomy department for nearly forty years. His first popular children's book was about Galileo. Among his many contributions to children's literature since, Rosen authored a number of illustrated books, such as *Where Does the Moon Go?*, *Can You Catch a Falling Star?*, *Which Way to the Milky Way?*, and *How Far Is a Star?* With his wife, Dorothy Rosen, he coauthored a mystery series featuring Belle Appleman, a Jewish immigrant from Boston's West End.

INTEGRATED MEDIA

Find a full list of our authors and
titles at www.openroadmedia.com

FOLLOW US
@OpenRoadMedia